the ***Topp Twins***
book

CW00822047

the Topp *Twins* book

Jools and Lynda Topp

PENGUIN BOOKS

PENGUIN BOOKS

Penguin Books (NZ) Ltd, cnr Airborne and Rosedale Roads, Albany,
Auckland 1310, New Zealand
Penguin Books Ltd, 80 Strand, London, WC2R 0RL, England
Penguin Putnam Inc, 375 Hudson Street, New York, NY 10014, United States
Penguin Books Australia Ltd, 250 Camberwell Road, Camberwell,
Victoria 3124, Australia
Penguin Books Canada Ltd, 10 Alcorn Avenue, Toronto,
Ontario, Canada M4V 3B2
Penguin Books (South Africa) (Pty) Ltd, 24 Sturdee Avenue, Rosebank,
Johannesburg 2196, South Africa
Penguin Books India (P) Ltd, 11, Community Centre, Panchsheel Park,
New Delhi 110 017, India
Penguin Books Ltd, Registered Offices: Harmondsworth, Middlesex, England

First published by Penguin Books (NZ) Ltd, 2003

1 3 5 7 9 10 8 6 4 2

Copyright © Jools and Lynda Topp 2003

The right of Jools and Lynda Topp to be identified as the authors of this
work in terms of section 96 of the Copyright Act 1994 is hereby asserted.

Designed by Seven
Printed by Condor Production, Hong Kong

All rights reserved. Without limiting the rights under copyright reserved above,
no part of this publication may be reproduced, stored in or introduced
into a retrieval system, or transmitted, in any form or by any means
(electronic, mechanical, photocopying, recording or otherwise), without
the prior written permission of both the copyright owner and
the above publisher of this book.

ISBN 0-14-301860-4
A catalogue record for this book is available from the National Library of New Zealand
www.penguin.co.nz

Contents

For Mum and Dad

Thank yous

This book could not have been written without the help of some very hardworking and dedicated people.

To all the folks at Penguin for their constant support and professional advice. Special thanks to our Penguin team: Geoff Walker, Louise Armstrong and Rebecca Lal.

To the guys at Seven who did a great job designing the book, thanks Paul and Gideon.

To our manager, Arani Cuthbert, who has been with us for more than ten years, thanks for believing we could write a book, dealing with all the paperwork and listening to and enduring numerous versions of our stories.

To Bambina for supplying the venue and fuel for everything from our first business meeting about the book to our final edit.

A really big hug and many thanks to Amy Isackson who spent months editing all of our stories and shaping them so you could understand them in her far away home in America. Thank heavens for computers.

And finally, to all our fans who have supported us over the years and, in a way, made this book possible.

Jean and Peter Topp.

Julie and Lynda were born to succeed. Their education started at Gordonton School and continued at Ruawaro. Then, both attended Huntly College where they showed sheer determination to progress. Julie and Lynda were successful in all sports but excelled at athletics and horse riding. Entertaining came naturally to them at a very early age, with their initiative to use a hairbrush as a microphone and a tennis racket as a guitar. When they were 12, Brother Bruce gave them a real guitar for Christmas and their performing career began. Over the years, Julie and Lynda have become two of the best known and loved entertainers in New Zealand and around the world. Their skills include singing, yodelling, acting and comedy. They've won many awards in all categories.

These two talented and loving country gals have made us, their parents, proud of them and all their achievements.

Love,

Mum and Dad

Growing Up

Jools & Lynda at six months, with Mum & Bruce

Jools and I were born in 1958 at the Huntly Maternity Hospital. We had shared a womb for nine months and on 14 May at 10 pm, Jools informed me that it was time to venture out. I was in no rush, content to lounge around for awhile, but Jools was adamant that it was time to go. She took off on the downhill run, so to speak, and popped out weighing four lbs. Think four blocks of good New Zealand butter. Everyone was expecting an eight pound baby.

The doctors went into emergency mode because four blocks of good New Zealand butter is too small for one good New Zealand baby, and they rushed Jools down the road to the chicken farm to be placed under the heat lamps.

Meanwhile, back in the womb, I was having a fabulous time. I had a cigarette and a martini and I would have stayed for the movie, but Mum must have felt me mixing my cocktail and informed the doctors that another baby was on the way. Five minutes after Jools, I popped out weighing a perfect four lbs, adding up to the eight lb baby Mum was supposed to have.

The doctors then decided that Jools was a good size for a twin and brought her back from the chicken farm to be united with Mum and me.

Right from the word go, Jools and I have only really been celebrated as twins. When we were little babies, old ladies would peer into our pram as our Mum and brother wheeled us into town and mutter, 'Gosh, there so alike', and 'Aren't they adorable?' Even now when we meet friends separately, their first question is usually, 'Where's your sister?'

Aged 2. Lynda and Jools with Santa.

At an early age, Jools and I realised that we could use the twin thing to our advantage. As soon as we had our own wheels, matching trikes at the age of three, we were fleecing the public of every available lolly and ice cream. We'd tell Mum that we were just going for a ride in the driveway and then, as soon as the coast was clear, we'd high-tail it into town to make the rounds. I suppose because we had each other we didn't worry about getting lost.

First stop was the doctor's office where she had a jar of lollies on the counter for sick children. We would stay just long enough to get a handful and then we'd go off down to the shop where we'd be given an ice cream just for being the twins. Last stop was the old lady on the way home who would give us morning tea before we headed back to a frantic Mum searching the driveway for her girls.

Some incidents from your childhood stay firmly fixed in your mind forever. These two stories from when we were kids are pretty weird, and we suppose that's why they've stayed with us.

You see, our schoolteacher happened to be what you'd call a 'pigeon fancier', and the idea that you could send birds off into the world to fly around for a while and that they'd come right back home just intrigued the hell out of Lynda and me. We decided to try and convince our parents that it would be invaluable to have our very own flock of world-class homing pigeons.

We told Mum that it would help us to keep in touch with her when we were out on the farm, that we could send her important messages from the back paddock like, 'We're heading home so you better put the jug on', or 'We've forgotten the pliers, can you bring them down to the boundary fence?' We're sure Mum would have waited patiently at the window watching for our messages to arrive by pigeon post.

When we told Dad about our fancy idea, he gave us a big fat no. Our interest in pigeons didn't fly with him. However, we were undeterred by his response and we nagged him for days to try and get him to change his mind. One night, after we finished helping milk the cows and whining that we didn't have homing pigeons, Dad asked us to carry out a strange task. He gave us a little matchbox and directed us to put the biggest, fattest, juiciest chook poo from the chook run in it and bring it up to the house. We thought the old man had flipped his lid but hurried off to fulfill his request and proudly handed over what we thought was the chook poo of the century.

Dad took a glass from the kitchen cupboard and filled it with fresh clean water from the tap. Then he carefully deposited the big old poo into the glass, swilled it around, banged it down on the bench and said very seriously, 'Okay, which one of you wants to drink this?'

We both said, 'There's no way we're drinking that.' And Dad just casually remarked, 'There'll be no more talk of pigeons then, will there?'

You see, we collected our drinking water from the roof of the house and Dad knew that the homing pigeons, even though they would have been a great hobby for his twins, would probably have spent most of their time perched on the roof, shitting in the gutter and making our beautiful clean rainwater undrinkable.

We reckon Dad still chuckles to himself over the chicken shit drink to this very day.

We didn't always get what we wanted when we were growing up, but one thing we did have was an old push-bike. She wasn't much to look at, but she was like gold to us. When you were free-wheeling down the hill she would turn into a pony from the wild west, or when you were riding through the swamp she became a dug-out canoe searching for a lost tribe in the Amazon.

But it's hard to have one bike and a set of twins. You see it never occurred to us to take turns riding that bike. So, we fought over it. Our rule was: whoever had the bike at the end of the day automatically got it the following morning. We spent our days trying to keep possession, no matter what.

One afternoon, I had the bike in my hot little hands and in order to keep it, rode about a mile from the house and hid it in long grass. The next morning, as the sun was rising over our house, I was already heading up the road in my pyjamas to reclaim the bike. I found it exactly where I had hidden it the night before and started to ride home.

Soon, I realised that Lynda had followed me up the road, and after some bickering and handlebar pulling, I got the leg of my new PJs stuck in the bike's chain. I was all caught up and no amount of tugging and swearing would release me. Lynda offered to help, but I was suspicious of her motives. I didn't want her thieving little paws anywhere near our bike. But, in the end, I had to let her push it as I put my arm around her neck for support and hopped on one leg home.

When we arrived Mum was furious at the state of my PJs and tried to free me without doing them more damage. However, her efforts failed and she had to cut the leg off with the scissors.

The thing that I remember most about that incident is that while Mum was performing surgery, both Lynda and I had a vice-like grip on the handlebars, ready to take possession as soon as I was freed. I'm not sure who ended up with the bike that day, but I do know that we both ended up with a sense of cunning and determination because of that old two-wheeler.

Mum, Dad, us kids and Aunty Gert's dog

As you can see, when we were five-years-old butter wouldn't melt in our mouths and we were the cutest kids on the block. We had a flair for fashion at an early age. In fact, we anticipated fashion trends and the streetwise gear we are pictured wearing here is still in style today, especially the three-quarter length pants.

In the photo below, I think Lynda is wearing brother Bruce's clothes and has adorned herself with Bruce's little cowboy pistol that she stole – evidence of her foreknowledge of cowboy chic.

We started our very own gang with this tomboy look. If my memory serves me right we called it 'Tikes on Trikes', predecessor to the eternally fashionable 'Dykes on Bikes' movement. We'd terrorise the neighbourhood in our boy-cut trousers with armed hold ups and cowboy-style shootouts. We spared no one, not even our poor mother, who had, by this stage, given up trying to get us into nice little dresses and just allowed us to wear whatever we wanted. She was one of those cool Mothers of the Sixties.

Getting ready to terrorise the neighbourhood

Lynda as Little Miss Muffet

Jools as Bo Peep

Hula Girls

Since 'Tikes on Trikes', our lives have been all about dressing up. Little Miss Muffet and Bo Peep were our first glamour characters, preceding Camp Mother and Camp Leader. They appeared at the age of six at Gordonton School Fancy Dress. The following year, we débuted our hula girl look, wearing dresses our Aunty Ruth had brought back for us from the Islands.

Camp Mother
and
Camp Leader emerge

If there is anyone in particular in our family who contributed to our becoming two of New Zealand's favourite entertainers, it is our brother Bruce. Bruce loved music when he was growing up. He played the piano by ear and loved to buy all the latest albums.

When Lynda, Bruce and I were at Huntly College together, we sang a song in the talent quest called 'Lean on Me' and won second place. We sang and Bruce did the harmony, because that's what Bruce did. If you sang him a note he'd always sing a harmony back to you.

While we thought this was pretty cool, there is one thing in particular that set us on the road to stardom that we thank Bruce for, even more than for his harmonies.

When we were 12, Bruce had a job up the road mowing the neighbour's lawn and for some beautiful unselfish reason he saved up his money and bought us a guitar and a book entitled *Play in a Day*. It was the best present ever and we really did play in a day. In fact, it's the only guitar tuition we ever had.

Bruce is now a florist and we think he is the most creative and talented one in our family. Yes, Bruce is gay too. We think there must have been something in the water.

And this is probably as good a time as any to thank Mum and Dad for allowing us all to discover our sexuality in our own good time and for accepting us and loving us through it all.

Here's to our beautiful brother.

Brother Bruce and us

Dunedin ⊙

There comes a time when all good twins must leave home. We were 17 when we decided to set off and see the world, and the South Island seemed like a great place for us to start.

We had no idea how we were going to get there, but we discovered that if you joined the Territorial Army, you got to train at Burnham Military Camp just outside Christchurch. So we enlisted and caught the cabbage train from Hamilton and headed off on an exciting new adventure.

We were the last group of women who trained together before the army integrated, and us gals had a great time learning the spoils of war. We developed a real camraderie making beds, polishing shoes, marching to meals and helping each other over the obstacle course.

After six weeks of intensive training we were scheduled to return home to join up with the Waikato unit, but we went AWOL in Christchurch and stayed there for two years. The Army wasn't the career we were looking for.

Untouchable girls

Our first big break in the music scene came in Christchurch. We played at an old coffee shop called The Victorian Coffee Lounge and we were paid $5 each plus as many toasted sandwiches as we could eat.

The Victorian was frequented by young radicals, hippie types with long hair and duffel coats, and women who called themselves feminists. We instantly felt at home with the more radical feminists who also called themselves lesbians.

Growing up we knew we were different, but we just didn't have a name for what we were. Once we met women who identified as lesbians, we thought, 'Oh, they're just like us.' We never went though any traumas about our sexuality, but instead started singing about it.

We created a name for ourselves at the Victorian and the owners of a bigger coffee lounge in Dunedin came to hear us sing. They liked what they heard and asked us to come and play for them every Thursday night.

We had a blast in Dunedin with lots of young university students who were a long way from home like us. We thought we were invincible.

Come 1977, most of our friends were heading off to the International Women's Convention in Hamilton. So, off we went too. We had joined the Revolution, and the women's army was marching. Good thing we'd practised back at Burnham Military Camp.

We sang at the Convention and became the darlings of the women's movement, with songs like 'Paradise' and 'We'll Fight For Our Freedom'. With our newfound fame we decided to move to Auckland, but we soon realised that living in the big city wasn't really our cup of tea. So we went bush. We moved out to a little wooden shack with no power at Te Henga, on the west coast.

We cooked outside on an open fire, wrote songs, collected mussels at the beach and watercress at the lake and worked for an old market gardener down the road who grew kumaras, garlic and the odd dope plant. We had three dogs and acquired our beautiful pet pig Gladys.

Living out on the west coast

One night we decided to go in to town to get some supplies and have a night out at the pub. We spent all our money – or should we say dole – on groceries before we realised that our beat-up old Holden Special was about as low on gas as you can get.

It just so happened that we had the guitar in the back of the car, so we headed down to Queen Street and sang our hearts out to earn some gas money. In about 20 minutes we made 150 bucks, which was the most money we had made in a couple of years. We were hooked.

Young Radicals busking

Every Friday night after that we packed up the car and headed into town to take Queen Street by storm. It was there on the sidewalk that we learned the art of entertaining: how to be spontaneous, involve the crowd, sing loudly, be funny and do anything that stopped passersby and got them to give us money. We attracted huge crowds and developed our own style of performance.

On 6 November 1989 it was just another Friday night and another show on Queen Street for us. Things were going well. A huge crowd had gathered round to watch our antics and listen to our latest political song. The guitar case was filling up with money and things were going well. Then, all of a sudden, there was a screech of tyres and we were surrounded by uniformed police officers. They tried to shut us down and asked the crowd to move on, but their sirens and flashing lights attracted even more people, causing the crowd to spill out into the street. Jools and I tried to reason with the police, but the crowd started booing and pelting the policemen with coins. After 15 minutes of this standoff, reinforcements arrived and two officers bundled Jools and me into the back of a police car. I can remember Jools yelling out to a friend of ours to rescue our dog and guitar that we left behind.

Young Radicals performing at Sweetwaters

The show which has packed out houses in Auckland, Huntly, Hamilton, Wellington, Nelson and Christchurch is coming your way soon!

PALMERSTON NORTH
Globe Theatre, Tues Nov 1 – Thurs Nov 3, 8PM
Book at Farmers Broadway, PH 86-382

NEW PLYMOUTH
State Insurance Theatre, Fri Nov 4, 8PM
Book at the Opera House, PH 84-947

MASTERTON
Wairarapa Arts Centre, Thurs Nov 10, 8PM
Book at the Arts Centre, PH 81-210

WELLINGTON
Return Season!
Downstage Theatre, Sun Nov 13, 5PM & 8PM
Book at Downstage, PH 849-639

HASTINGS
New Playhouse Theatre, Wed Nov 16, 8PM
Book Foster Brook, Heretaunga St West, PH 89-204

NAPIER
Century Theatre, Thurs Nov 17, 8PM
Book Century Theatre, PH 57-781

GISBORNE
Lawson Field Theatre, Fri Nov 18, 8PM
Book Tattersal & Bailey, Gladstone Rd, PH 76-507

ROTORUA
Rotorua Art Gallery, Sat Nov 19, 8PM
Book Art Gallery, PH 85-594

TAURANGA
Kumara Shed, Works Rd, Katikati, Sat Dec 10, 8PM
Book Arts Council Tauranga, Just Hers Katikati

WHANGAREI
Forum North, Thurs Dec 15, 8PM
Book Forum North, PH 84-879

Presented by Brian Sweeney's Agency, P.O. Box 19016, Wellington.

"The greatest original talent emerging in New Zealand."
NZ Herald

The TOPP TWINS

"The greatest original talent emerging in New Zealand!"
NZ Herald

PRESENT THEIR NEW SHOW

TOPP SECRET

TURN OVER FOR THE 'TOPP SECRET' DETAILS!

Topp Secret flyer

Jools and I felt sure that the police would take us around the corner, drop us off and tell us to piss off home. But instead, we got the whole treatment. They took us to the Watch Tower, fingerprinted and photographed us, charged us with obstruction and threw us into the cells for the night. We were released at 5 am and ordered to appear in court the following day.

Jools and I decided to act as our own counsel and arrived in court wearing suits and carrying briefcases. This was our first character performance.

We argued against the charge of obstruction. Our defence: that the crowd obstructed the footpath not us, and therefore we should be acquitted on a technicality.

The judge was not persuaded by our argument and the prosecution called six witnesses to the stand. The usual questioning and cross-examination ensued, which took most of the day. Then Jools and I played our trump card: a letter from Dame Cath Tizard, the then Mayor of Auckland, stating that she loved our music and couldn't wait to hear us on Queen Street next Friday night.

We broke for recess and Jools and I ate our lunches out of our briefcases. The judge returned and issued his verdict. He defended the police's actions that night, but said we bought life and excitement to downtown Auckland and came up with a plan that still stands today. If Jools and I go busking, we must ring the Central Police Station and they have to supply two uniformed police officers to assist with crowd control.

While we were relieved that we weren't heading for the slammer, the judge's plan took the spontaneity out of busking for us. Luckily, the Students Art Council had offered us our first national tour, anyway. So we headed off to wow New Zealand.

Young Radicals

The Student Arts Council Tour was a great success. We got booked to perform at the first Sweetwaters, we started performing in theatres, and the dressing up began. The Ginghams and Raelene and Brenda made their débuts at the Gods at the old, and now sadly gone, Mercury Theatre. We were on a roll. Our careers were taking off.

TOPP TWINS
at Mercury II
18-28 July

A new show from the singing sisters!

Provocative, vibrant and very, very funny.
See the Topp Twins in the intimacy of Mercury II.

Not-to-be-missed entertainment.

Twelve shows only!

Performance Times

Wed, 18, 6.15pm
Thu 19, 9.15pm
Fri 20, 6.15pm
Sat 21, 6.15pm
Sun 22, 4.00pm

Tue 24, 6.15pm
Wed 25, 6.15pm
Thu 26, 9.15pm
Fri 27, 6.15pm
Sat 28, 6.15 & 11pm

Please phone 33-869 to reserve your seats - NOW!
Pin this leaflet next to your telephone so you can tell your friends about the Topp Twins' season at Mercury II.

Photo by Bruce Connew
Presented by **Brian Sweeney**, P.O. Box 19016 Wellington.

Mercury flyer

23

Name
Camp Mother

Born
Happy Valley

School
Correspondence School

Favourite food
Scones with good New Zealand butter

Favourite song
'I did it my way'

Most like to meet
The Queen

Achievements
Too numerous to write, but I would have to say one of my greatest achievements has been the profile I have brought to camping in New Zealand.

Desires
To one day run this great country as Prime Minister

I have had a privileged and happy career. In fact, I don't see what I do as a job, but more as my life's work. I have been running camping grounds for many many years now, along with my right hand woman Camp Leader, and am constantly reminded of the joy and happiness the parking of a caravan or the pegging of a tent brings. I know that over the years I have become more than a Camping Ground Supervisor to most of you, through my many appearances on T.V and, of course, through the role I play in the fashion world with my many and varied Jumpsuits. To me, Camping and Jumpsuits go hand in hand. They are two of New Zealand's greatest summer traditions, and I have dedicated my life to maintaining them in this country and promoting them to the rest of the world.

CM for PM!

Must go, I have a batch of scones in the oven.

Camp Mother

Name

Camp Leader

Born

Abandoned in public toilets and found by Mother Superior of the Little Sisters of the Poor

School

Little Sisters of the Poor Convent School for wayward and abandoned children

Favourite food

Orange or lime jelly

Favourite song

'You are my sunshine'

Most like to meet

Judy Bailey

Achievements

Received all my Brownie Badges and played lead recorder in the school orchestra

Desires

To have laser treatment so I don't have to wear glasses

My name means a lot to me. A leader is a person who shows the way, is a good example to the community and is not afraid to try anything unless it is dangerous. I think I have been a great influence on the young people of New Zealand and keeping the cardigan fashion alive is just one example of my being a person who is not afraid to show the way. Camp Mother is my best friend. She knows everything and can fix anything with the contents of her handbag. My job is to help Camp Mother fulfill her dreams. One day I think she will be awarded the NZ Service Medal for her services to camping. I love NZ. I think it's the best place in the world even though I have never been anywhere else; it has great people, beautiful beaches, wide-open spaces and cheap jelly sandals.

Camp Leader

This is me standing outside our beloved little caravan. It was built in 1956 and is called a 'Starlet', which is sort of like me on our television programmes. Camp Mother says she's the star but I don't mind 'cos she's really good at what she does.

We have had the best holidays in our caravan. We've been to every caravan park in New Zealand and have met some amazing people along the way. Once Camp Mother prepared dinner for 16 people in the Starlet. She made my favourite dish, 'Lamb's brains on a bed of tripe in a white sauce'. She says it's a really difficult dish to make in a caravan and we all ate outside 'cos you can only get two people in a Starlet at a time. And even then you have to be at either end of the caravan, otherwise she tips up. Once I forgot and over she went. Me and Camp Mother and our tea and scones all ended up pinned against the back window.

Even with just the two of us weighted properly, the Starlet is still a little crowded inside. Camp Mother insists on having at least 15 different outfits at all times, just in case there's a formal occasion she has to attend. I don't mind though 'cos I love the caravanning life, and I can get by with just one dress and my trusty green cardy.

You have to have a really good attitude if you go caravanning 'cos lots of things can go wrong. Once I forgot to put the safety chain on. We were going around one of those sharp bends in the Karangahake Gorge and the Starlet got the wobbles. She snapped off the car and beat us to Waihi by five minutes. You have to remain calm in situations like that, and caravan folks always do. Camp Mother says people who own caravans are less likely to have heart attacks than those who don't.

I always change the tyre on the Starlet when we get a flat. My other job, which I'm real good at, is levelling her up once she's parked. Camp Mother hates being on a lean. She says it's bad for your circulation and that's why lots of people have varicose veins.

This year we are going to go to the Invercargill Camping Ground to join up with the South Island Caravanning and Handknitters' Association. Camp Mother says people who knit are ten times less likely to get arthritis than those who don't. I can't wait to pack up the Starlet, hook her up to the Bambina and head off on another exciting adventure.

Happy caravanning!

Camp Leader

Camp Leader with the Starlet

There's nothing I like better than to whip up a batch of scones for morning tea. You can't beat them for simplicity or taste.

I prefer a plain scone, but some people add cheese or dates. If you have guests over, a Devonshire Tea is always impressive. Whipped cream and strawberry jam on scones is pure heaven.

Whichever way you choose to prepare them, always serve your scones hot from the oven and use good New Zealand butter.

You will need:

8 oz self-raising flour

1 level tspn baking powder

Good shake salt

1 oz castor sugar

1/4 pint milk

2 oz good New Zealand butter

Sift flour, baking powder and salt. Rub butter into dry mixture with your hands. This is important, as the warmth of your hands softens the butter.

Add sugar.

Mix to a soft dough with the milk. Turn on to a floured board and knead quickly.

Don't finger it too much or you'll lose the light fluffy texture.

Pat out dough. Cut into rough squares with a wet knife.

Place on a hot baking tray. You can brush the tops with milk to make them go golden brown.

Bake in a hot oven at 450F for 12 to 15 minutes.

Scones are delicious served with jam, honey or golden syrup. Always serve scones with a cup of tea and, if it's summertime, take morning tea on the porch.

Camp Mother is probably the best cook in New Zealand, but I think that I make the best Jellied Sandals in the world.

You will need:

One clean jelly sandal
(preferably one of the glitter variety)

2 pkts lime-green jelly

1 banana

1 pkt Smarties

1 pkt hundreds and thousands

Scrub the jelly sandal so that it's spotless, concentrating on the underside of the shoe where the little grips gather mud and dog poo. Do up the buckle and place in a glass bowl – this is your feature for the jelly pudding.

In another bowl, mix the jelly crystals with hot water and follow the directions on the packet.

Allow the mixture to cool, and then pour the jelly over the sandal, making sure to cover it. Caution: Cooling the jelly is very important. Pouring boiling hot jelly is not only dangerous but will melt the sandal into a sticky blob.

Place in the fridge to set. Once your jelly is set, cut the banana into slices and arrange on top of the jelly like daisy petals, leaving a hole in the centre. Fill the hole with Smarties.

Sprinkle hundreds and thousands right around the edge of the bowl. Place the bowl on the table so everybody can see your beautiful jelly sandal set in jelly.

Serve with fruit salad and ice cream. Yum.

During the 50s and 60s, the jumpsuit was New Zealand's favourite summer fashion, but it was pushed to the back of the closet in the 70s by paisley tops and bell bottoms. Not one to be swayed by fly-by-night fashions, I stayed with the jumpsuit and have elevated it to even greater heights than it enjoyed in its heyday. I have designed jumpsuits for every occasion using exotic fabrics from around the world.

Jumpsuits are comfortable, practical, glamorous, sophisticated and equally acceptable for both day and evening wear. Anyone can put on the jumpsuit, but an ample bosom is required to keep it in place. A contrasting handbag

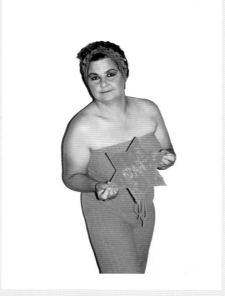

Here's me in the pink.

is a must, and carrying your handbag at the correct height to accentuate the bosom is just as important. Follow my **HILWN** method: **H**andle **I**n **L**ine **W**ith **N**ipple. Panty line must also never be visible and, of course, a matching turban sets off the whole ensemble.

Pictured here are some of my favourite jumpsuits created by my dressmaker extraordinaire, Terri Lynne Towelling.

JUMPSUIT
International

"My Favourite Jumpsuits"

Evening Wear

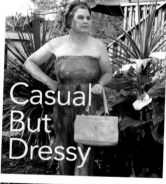

Casual But Dressy

Highland Fling

amp Mother
ashion Icon

As a young gal I was very active. I could hardly wait to finish my correspondence school lessons each day, don rompers and blouse and head outside. I spent many an afternoon playing sports and even now, the smell of liniment in the gals changing rooms sends a shiver through my bosom.

We, as women, have come a long way from the days of knee-length sport and bathing costumes that dominated my teenage years, and we are making our presence felt in what were once considered men's games, such as rugby, golf and, of course, polo.

It's great to see young women enjoying their sport in their trendy new costumes, but I must stress the importance of the brassiere when participating in vigorous activity.

I, myself, find it very difficult to enjoy a few chukkas on the polo field without the support of my trusty D-cup, lift and separate, hold-them-all-in sports bra. I can tell you that charging down a polo field at 30-odd kilometres an hour with flying ta-tas is not only dangerous but seriously impedes your chances of getting a good swing at the ball. So, heave ho and away you go.

Keep up the good work, all you sporty gals! Love and support,

Camp Mother

Here we are getting ready to train with the New Zealand Army Reserves.
Camp Mother and I are in charge of the catering corp. We must get
cups of tea and hot scones through to the front line for morning and
afternoon tea, no matter what.

On our training exercises, Camp Mother makes me crawl over 10
miles of rugged terrain with my bulletproof tea urn. I can do it in just
over six hours without spilling a drop. Camp Mother is with me all
the way, yelling encouragement and urging me on from her armoured
personnel carrier. Once I got caught in a barbed wire fence and the tap
on the urn opened up, and I got very bad scalds on the back of my
legs, but still arrived in time for morning tea with just enough hot
water. Camp Mother bandaged my burns from her first aid kit and
said I was a credit to the catering corp.

Over and Out!

Camp Leader

35

The Famous Green Cardy, knitter unknown, bought
by Camp Mother at the Op Shop for one dollar.

One of the most amazing things that has happened since my rise to
fame is the willingness of the New Zealand public to help dress me.
Over the years, hundreds of Kiwis have sent me sensational hand
knitted items which you can see pictured on the opposite page.

I would like to take this opportunity to thank all the generous and
talented people who have made things for me and tell you about my
love of handknitted items.

Camp Mother gave me my first cardigan, my green 'I Love New
Zealand' cardy, which has become my most treasured possession. I
wear that cardy everywhere. I've climbed mountains in it, shorn sheep
in it, used it as my jockey colours while galloping a thoroughbred
racehorse past the winning post and worn it to many formal occasions.

The humble NZ Cardy takes its place of honour in this country
along with crocheted doilies, pom-pom poodle toilet roll covers and
lace tissue box holders. All these items are practical but none can
outdo the cardigan. Easy to slip on as well as fashionable, it has kept
my kidneys warm on many a cold winter's night.

Camp Mother says you can have endless years of enjoyment from
your cardy if you just take a little time to care for it properly. I always
hand wash mine with recommended soap and lay flat on a towel to dry.

Black cardy
The Black Three-dimensional Cardy, knitter
unknown and gifted by Felicity Garland.

Black cardy; rear view
Back of three-dimensional cardy.

White cardy
The Natural Merino Wool Cardy, knitted and gifted
by Heather Kerr of ECOBITI Handknits.

Blue cardy
The Kiwi Cardy knitted and gifted by
Mrs Ngaire Lambourne of Wainuiomata

Presented to

Camp Leader

for

her tireless dedication to Camp Mother

I would just like to say a few words about my right-hand woman, Camp Leader. Over the years she has been behind me in all my ventures. She is always willing, whether it's carrying enormous amounts of camping gear on our holidays, or carrying me, as seen in this picture. Camp Leader has, of course, become a household name due to the enormous popularity of my television programmes, but she has never ever got above her station in life, and is always happy to concentrate her energy into making my life just that much easier.

I remember the time fondly when Camp Leader saved me from certain death, when a flock of sheep had become confused and disorientated and she threw herself between the angry mob and me. Camp Leader was trampled by 3000 merinos that day, but I was protected by her heroic efforts.

All in all, Camp Leader is a great friend and I shall always be grateful for her undying loyalty to me.

Camp Mother

Put the jug on Camp Leader, I'd love a cup of tea.

CAMP LEADER COMPETES IN THE IRONMAN TRIATHLON

CAMP MOTHER GIVES CAMP LEADER LAST MINUTE INSTRUCTIONS AT THE START OF THE IRONMAN

CONT.

Never ever poke a wasps' nest with a stick.

Never ever lick the inside of the freezer.

Never ever pretend to be a parachute jump instructor.

Never ever climb a power pole and attach a kiddies' swing
to the power lines.

Never ever tie yourself to a Spanish fighting bull.

Never ever plant a cactus garden at a McDonald's playground.

Never ever ride a motorcycle backwards.

Never ever lock yourself in the car with a skunk.

Never ever dry your hair in a spin dryer.

Never ever use grated chilies as a party dip.

Never ever have a picnic on an international runway.

Never ever try to warm up your Chihuahua in a microwave.

Never ever use a boa constrictor as a washing line.

Never ever nominate your mother in a nude wrestling match.

Never ever perform open-heart surgery, unless you're a doctor.

Name
Raelene

Born
Henderson Maternity

School
Henderson Valley High

Favourite food
Egg burger

Favourite Song
'Shut up a your face'

Achievements
Yeah lots

Desires
Yeah lots

I had an unhappy childhood but then I met Brenda at Henderson Valley High and my whole life changed. Me and Brenda were inseparable and then together we discovered boys, burgers and the speedway. Me and Brenda flat together now in a real neat state house in Henderson. I'm doing work experience at a hair salon and one day I hope to open a salon with Brenda. We've already got the name –'Cuts for Sluts' – neat eh?

Raelene & Brenda

Name
Brenda

Born
Invercargill, moved to Te Atatu South at the age of 14

School
Invercargill Primary – expelled Henderson Valley High

Favourite food
Hot dog

Favourite song
'I'm too sexy for my shirt'

Achievements
Still working on them

Desires
Wayne and Neil

I grew up in Invercargill where my parents ran the local takeaway bar, so at an early age I had a passion for fast cars and fast food. And when I was fourteen our family moved to West Auckland where I meet my best friend Raelene. We'd meet at Henderson Mall every Friday night and then we'd go to the Speedway, the Take A Way bar, and end up at one of my boyfriend's parties. I was the first girl in my class to get breasts and a boyfriend and on my birthday, he gave me a pair of ug boots, it was the neatest present ever, eh. I don't think its really necessary to have an education, like I know everything there is to know about make-up and they don't teach you anything like that in class. Raelene wants to start a beauty salon but if it never gets off the ground I reckon we could get a job as exotic dancers real easy cos we dance all the time at parties and we're both really good looking.

Brenda & Wanye
Up a Tree
KISSING

Brent, one of our boyfriends, says the foundations of a house are the most important things when he's building. Well, it's the same with make-up. Foundation is like the most important ingredient. It's where you start. And after you've finished applying your liquid or powder foundation it's just layer upon layer upon layer of blusher, concealer, mascara, eyeliner, lipstick and the finishing touches like your glitter and eyelash extensions.

Brenda is like an artist. She can start off with a girl who's got a really poxy face and you wouldn't even recognise her after Brenda's done her makeover. One of Brenda's specialties is covering pimples. She says you've got to blend them away and it just comes naturally to her.

All our girlfriends love it when we have make-up parties. Everybody brings all their stuff over and we all try each other's make-up. The guys all roll their eyes when we have our parties but secretly they love it, 'cos it's for them, eh.

You do have to be careful though. One time we had this really bad outbreak of herpes after using Sheryl Johnston's lipstick. It was okay though 'cos it wasn't the sexual disease – talk about lucky.

So don't be afraid to paint that beautiful face of yours, remember our make-up motto: 'Your choice – foxy or poxy'.

Me and Brenda heading to Wallington for the weekend

Sometimes Raelene and me have to go further than the mall. Below are our tips for travelling further than 500 metres:

Always look your best 'cos lots of people are going to see you.

Make sure you wear bright colours so you don't get run over.

Stockings are really good when you're walking 'cos they stop you from getting chafing on the insides of your thighs.

Don't yell at people if they slow down and then take off. They're probably just trying to get a pattern off your outfit.

Like in our photo, wear really high shoes so you have better vision.

Never run after a car. Running is only for when you're being chased.

Finally, and most importantly, if some one stops, **never** get in the car. Hitching is about being seen, not getting somewhere.

Everyone loves a party and when there's lots of booze around, it's a really good idea to have food, otherwise people start puking up on your purple shag pile. So here's some of our fave party snacks.

First off, you have to have chips and dips, 'cos it's the sign of a really good hostess and it soaks up alcohol and you don't need plates. Another dish you can make is cheese and pineapple on toothpicks stuck in an orange cut in half – this one is easy to make but looks really exotic on the table. If you want something more substantial, you can do saveloys on a plate with tomato sauce. Everyone loves this dish and it's really good for you.

Sometimes if we think the party is going to go on for a few days we'll put on a big pot of savoury mince – 'cos this is the type of dish that can be used as dinner or breakfast. Neat, eh! Neil, one of our boyfriends, thinks this is real clever and he usually eats most of it, so you've got to be quick when he's around.

If you're really artistic like us you can have a theme party. One time we had a party and you had to come as your favourite big-time wrestler. We thought it would be a good idea to incorporate food in our theme so we made a whole lot of jelly so the girls could wrestle in it. Jelly went everywhere in the lounge, but you can suck most of it up if you hire one of those wet and dry vacuums.

Recipe For Big-Time Jelly Wrestling

Get heaps of jelly packets from the supermarket
Boil lots of water
Make the jelly in, like, plastic buckets
Let the jelly set but not too hard
Blow up a kid's paddling pool
Tip in jelly
Add two girls
Wrestle

People just love coming to our parties and we think its 'cos we put a lot of effort and thought into the kinds of food we prepare. See you at our next one, eh!

Me and Raelene go to the speedway every Saturday night. We used to just walk around and check out the cars and the boys, but we both felt we needed more. Raelene had this really neat idea for us to get more involved and now we walk around selling hotdogs and chips. Raelene and me came up with this really neat chant, 'Hurry, hurry, get 'em quick. Hotdogs, popcorn, sausage on a stick.' The Speedies, that's what we call the spectators, just love it when we come by.

We get our sausages from Frank. He has a caravan at the entrance to the pits called V-Ate. He does the best food at the speedway and hasn't missed a Saturday in 16 years. Frank does sausages, hotdogs and chips, and people just rush us when they know we've got Frank's sausages in our hot boxes. We reckon its 'cos Frank cooks everything in pure fat. A lot of the new food caravans use oil and it just doesn't taste the same.

You get to meet really interesting people when you're in the retail business and we've really got good at knowing our market. When we first started selling we would just walk around and wait for people to order from us, but now Raelene and I can take one look at a guy and know whether he's after a sausage or chips. Most of our clients usually order both 'cos we've just got that knack for selling. A lot of it is in the way you stand and your attitude. Like if you look at a guy and say 'Well do you want a sausage or not?' you're more likely to sell than if you say, 'What can I get you sir?' It's just little things like that that makes the difference between, like, $2 or nothing.

It's really good to have a hobby, eh. Brenda and me are drum majorettes for the Te Atatu Highland Pipe Band. I've been in the band since I was five, but Brenda has just joined.

Come on Brenda, hold your knockers up like this or you'll never get a good bang.

Brenda's flipped out, how embarrassing.

"The bands going the wrong way! Let's go and get a burger."

Brenda knows all the number one hits in Scotland . . . and the number twos.

Me and Raelene think war is really dumb 'cos you meet interesting people, but then you have to kill them. Like, they might be really spunky and go partying and clubbing just like we do, but you'd never get to go out with them, because you'd have to shoot them instead, eh.

Even though war sucks, we think the army is really amazing 'cos you can get a lot of boyfriends really easily. Like when we did our basic training at Waiouru, the guys were really neat and they helped us over the obstacle course and everything.

The hardest thing about the army was carrying our big packs around. But when we found out it can increase your bust by, like, two sizes we just went for it, eh? 'Cos sometimes you have to go through a bit of pain to look really beautiful.

There's one thing we reckon the army should change though. They should stop marching. Like, what's that for? They've got all those tanks and landrovers and helicopters and ships and you still have to walk everywhere – duh!

They also need to get with it and update their wardrobe, green and brown are really boring. There should be, like, six different outfits with shoes to go with each.

Most of the girls we trained with were in the army for a career. They weren't even interested in the guys. Lessos.

Anyway, we didn't mind 'cos it meant we had our pick of all the spunks.

Here's a really neat game you can play at your party.

You need 12 playing cards: lay them out on the floor like the face of a clock and put a bottle in the middle. Everybody sits around in a circle and takes turns at spinning the bottle. When the bottle stops spinning and points to a card, look in the book to see what the position you got means.

Kiss the person to your right. No tongues.

You are the sexiest person in the room - everyone gives you 50 cents.

Dance like a go-go dancer.

You have to sing a song.

You are the best dancer - get a foot massage from the person opposite you.

You have to make the dip for the next party.

Impersonate your favourite Topp Twins character.

Hop on one leg around the outside of the circle barking like a dog.

Wearing a blindfold on the lipstick on the person to your left.

Spin the bottle again.

Next time you go to a takeaway bar, you have to eat a tofu burger.

Play air guitar.

R&B Home Brew

55

Name
Ken Moller

Born
Wairapa Maternity Ward

School
Wairapa College. Was a shy boy but excelled in rugby.
Left school with no qualifications at age 15.

Favourite Food
Mutton with Mashed Potatoes and Leeks in White Sauce

Favourite Song
'Ten Guitars'

Most like to meet
The Lady in Pink

Achievements
Played first division rugby for Wairapa Bush, as hooker; Top breeder of Merino sheep;
Won the NZ Dog Trials with Bess in 1975

Desires
To sweep Camp Mother off her feet.

I'm a man of few words, and when I was asked to write this book I had the shits for a week.
But my best mate Ken Smythe came round to my place and encouraged me to talk about my life.

Well, I can tell you this country boy never dreamed he'd be a writer or hit the big time as
a television star. But, I know that deep down I'll always be remembered as a farmer, a hooker,
a dog man and a lover. And that's just fine by me.

The Lady In Pink has made me a very happy man. I will love her until the day I die, and
I hope to meet her before I do. She's bloody gorgeous.

Name
Ken Smythe

Born
Queen's Birthday Weekend
at National Women's

School
Mt. Albert Boys Grammar, excelled in poetry
and played the oboe in the school orchestra

Favourite Food
Macaroni Cheese (Bachelor's Casserole)

Favourite Song
'Dancing Queen' by Abba

Most like to meet
Dame Edna Everidge

Achievements
Master of Ikebana, the art of Japanese floral arrangement

Desires
To be the best man at Ken's wedding

A lot of people don't know this about me, but I have travelled extensively around the globe and feel this has made me a worldly type of man.

I have walked the Great Wall of China, swum the English Channel, climbed a third of the way up Mt Everest, travelled across the Mojave Desert by camel, and danced the men's dance of the native Galoombie tribe in deepest darkest Africa.

While I have enjoyed myself, I have realised that there is no greater place in the world than Ken Moller's lounge. For all my adventures taught me that a man without a friend is like a King without a Queen.

Ever since my grandfather, Billy Moller, threw me up on his 17-hand racehorse, slapped it on the ass and yelled out, 'Hang on boy', I've had an affinity with man's greatest love – the powerful and beautiful horse.

That first ride was a bit of a white knuckler for a five-year-old, but after 16 miles, two broken gates, a number of unscheduled jumps the scale of the Grand National, a hysterical and sobbing mother, and a near fatal car collision, I was still hanging on for grim life . . . and then me and the horse just clicked. It was like we were as one. Of course, back in those days, that's how everybody learnt to ride.

Nowadays times have changed. People have learnt that the powerful horse is actually a sensitive wee thing that has its own way of communicating. And a few of us lucky ones have tapped into this unique equine language called 'horse whispering'.

Actually, for years after that first ride people called me 'the Horse Mutterer'. Spurred on by my nickname, I developed my own horse language. I myself call it 'mare mumbling' and it is made up of a series of mumbles that I find myself muttering whenever I'm around these four-legged beauties.

See, back when the old thoroughbred bolted on me, I started yelling at the animal to whoa and when that didn't work, I screamed every swear-word I'd learnt as a five-year-old. After two hours of yelling 'whoa ya big shit', and 'bloody slow down, ya great hunk of dog tucker' and 'bugger, bugger, bugger', my swearing turned into a kind of melodic chant that was like a lullaby to that horse. And together, him and me, we made our way back to safety.

From that day on I've been able to talk with these animals, so to speak, and have been humbled by these intelligent and spirited creatures.

While strolling along in Japan, on one of my many overseas trips, I stumbled upon a grand college called 'Ikenobo'. Well that tickled my fancy because Ken is my name and I played the oboe in the school orchestra. After conversing with a local (luckily I speak fluent Japanese) I discovered that Ikenobo is where ikebana, the fascinating Oriental art of arranging cut stems, began hundreds of years ago. I also learned that Ikenobo, translated literally, means, 'hut by the pond'.

That set me to thinking about my best mate, Ken, who has a hut by the pond, a duck-shooting maimai on the edge of the swamp that he calls his little oasis. Ken rebuilds his maimai every shooting season and can't wait to crouch inside it with his quacker.

I went down to Ken's maimai once. It was a cold May morning and I was rugged up in my new cashmere sweater and merino gloves. I was about to take a sip of my hot Milo when Ken let go at a flock of birds with both barrels of his shotgun. Knocked back by the recoil, Ken flew into me and I was catapulted out the back of the maimai and landed in the swamp. A dead duck dropped from the sky onto me and I was then unceremoniously dragged back to the maimai by Ken's loyal gun dog.

When I returned to the warmth of my bed sit that afternoon, I realised that Ken's maimai is exactly the type of natural setting we are trying to create with ikebana. Remember the fundamental idea of an ikebana arrangement is to represent Heaven, Mankind and Earth. In 'My Maimai Arrangement', I chose special stems to represent these elements.

Trimmed swamp reeds spray out the side of a low container to represent the earth. A vibrant red hot poker tilted at a 45-degree angle represents Ken's rifle and a magnificent bird of paradise represents the low flying duck, heaven to a hunter like Ken. Finally, a little nut pod just beginning to open dangles over the side of the container and represents Ken, who is a fine example of mankind.

Ikebana is a great way for those of us who are not so well suited to life in the great outdoors to enjoy a bit of nature in the comfort of our own homes.

As a bachelor of many years, I have taught myself the art of impressing the ladies by turning out culinary delights such as 'Grilled Kidneys with Brussel Sprouts in Cheese Sauce' and 'Fish Finger Casserole'.

But my all-time favourite menu, which I would offer up to my lovely Lady in Pink, is a combination of Kiwi and Middle Eastern origins. In her role as a camping ground supervisor, my lovely lady comes into contact with people from all over the world and this dish would tantalise her international taste buds. Yes, I am talking about my signature dish:

'Pilau of Mutton with Veggie Ring',
followed by 'Gooseberry Batter Pudding'

I am giving you the recipe for this love potion and hope you have as much fun with it as I do.

Veggie Ring

1 lb mashed spuds	2 lb cooked diced veggies
Grated cheese	Salt

Form a ring of the hot mashed spuds on a fireproof dish.

Fill the centre with hot diced veggies, sprinkle the top with salt and grated cheese.

Brown under the grill for 5–10 minutes.

Ken & Ken

62

Pilau Of Mutton

1 lb mutton	1 pint mutton stock
3 oz rice	Cinnamon
Cloves	Salt
Knob of butter	2 onions

After killing your sheep and hanging it for two days, choose a piece from the loin. Wipe it carefully and trim off some of the fat. Put the mutton into a saucepan with the stock and stew till tender.

Now is probably a good time to set the table for two with placemats, candles and a small flower arrangement. Make sure the flower arrangement is short enough so that it will not interfere with the view of your date when you're seated at the table.

Back in the kitchen, lift the mutton out of the pan and put it to one side. Wash the rice and sprinkle it into the stock in which the mutton was cooked. Add the spices and salt. Don't be scared here. A lot of men hold back on the spices, but I have found a heavy-handed spice man is already at first base with a cultured and tasteful lady friend.

Let the rice simmer very slowly till cooked. Add the knob of butter and allow it to soak into the rice.

Cut the mutton into pieces and fry till golden brown in a little butter, then serve embedded in the rice. Garnish with fried onions.

This is my favourite way to prepare a pilau, but there are many different methods. The kind of meat, spices and garnish may be varied. Sometimes sultanas are added to the rice and hard-boiled eggs or meatballs may be used as a garnish.

Don't forget to wear a snazzy suit and serve the pilau with a warm stout. Guaranteed to knock her off her feet.

Gooseberry Batter Pudding

1 lb gooseberries	2 eggs
Half pint of milk	4 oz flour
Pinch of salt	Shavings of butter
Sugar to sweeten	Brown sugar to serve

Prepare the fruit. Sieve the flour and salt. Add some sugar. Make a well in the centre and add beaten eggs. Mix well. Add the milk and beat thoroughly. Stir in the gooseberries. Pour the whole lot into a greased bowl and steam for two hours. Serve in pudding bowls with butter and brown sugar sprinkled on top.
Bloody beautiful.

Ken Moller thinks that worker bees are the most romantic little fellas in the world. They spend all their time buzzing around their Queen answering to her every whim. And, he once said to me that he felt like a worker bee when he thought of his lovely Lady in Pink.

Old Kenny boy has been a bee man for years and whenever a wild swarm takes up residence in someone's prized garden, he's the first person they call. I went out with Ken once to watch him deal with a particularly angry bunch of Italian bees. There was a huge swarm of them on a kiwifruit vine in Bill and Judy Dalziel's backyard. Ken decided to bag them and asked me, of course, to hold the bag, which I did. 'Just slip the bag over the whole lot of them and then I'll hit the vine with a piece of four-by-two', he said. Before I could hightail it out of there, he had done just that. Most of the bees did drop into the bag, except for about 100 or so that were really not impressed and started attacking me.

The farmer's wife saw what was happening and she ran and got her kid's pram, filled it full of newspapers, set the thing on fire and came racing down the hill. Now, not only did I have a bag of over 1000 bees to hang onto and 100 or so trying to kill me, but I also had a firebomb pushed by a wailing banshee warrior woman heading directly for me. She had a rolled up newspaper in her hand and, as she neared the battle scene, started whacking me over the head with it so that the bees wouldn't get stuck in my hair. The smoke from the fiery pram did the trick, calming the bees down enough for me to get out of there with my life intact. Of course Ken Moller, as soon as he'd hit the bees, took off for the safety of the ute and was having a good giggle at my expense.

What Judy Dalziel did that day was the bravest thing I've ever seen anyone do and I promised her a big jar of honey from Ken's next harvest.

Goddess

Oh the first time I saw you
I nearly fainted on the spot
You hit me like my Nana's scones
Soft and round and hot

Oh my heart did a flip
And I thought my ticker had done its dash
Gees I was lovesick
And I broke out in a rash

Oh I love my country
And Ken is my best mate
But there comes a time
When a man has reached his prime
And hankers for a date

I'll put on my best shirt
And I'll wear a suit and tie
I'll buy you a bunch of flowers
And wipe the sleep out of my eyes
I'd do anything for you
I'd even wash my hair
I'd de-flea the old dog
And put on clean underwear

Oh how I love you
You are my missing link
You're a vision in my water trough
You're my Goddess bathed in Pink

Most of you know I'm an old romantic and I think writing a love letter is a great way to let that special lady in your life know how much she really means to you. Below I've provided you with a few words to help you write a love letter to your leading lady. Just fill in the blanks, cut it out and post it. For that extra touch of romance, I put a copy of my love poem on the back of your letter.

Dear . . . .

I love you like my favourite dog because...

My heart races like a hotted-up Ford Cortina when...

The way you flutter your eyes like a big jersey cow makes me feel...

When you preen yourself like a clucky hen I'd like to...

You're bloody gorgeous!

Love and kisses

from . . . .

As a young boy I spent many hours making things: little balsa wood gliders, trolleys and once I even made a ship in a bottle. But the toy I loved the most was a farm tractor I made from one of my mother's old cotton reels.

Here's how to make it. You will need:

1 cotton reel
1 rubber band a little bit longer than the cotton reel
1 matchstick
1 half of a matchstick
1 piece of household candle cut to 1cm with the wick removed.

With a small pocket knife, cut little notches around the edges of the cotton reel. This improves your tractor's traction on rough terrain. Ask Mum or Dad to help you when using any sharp objects like scissors or pocket knives. Never use your dad's skinning knife.

Push the rubber band through the hole in the cotton reel and through the candle where you took the wick out.

Push the half matchstick through the rubber band at the end of the cotton reel to hold it in place.

Now push the longer matchstick through the rubber band at the other end where the candle is. You can put a knot in the rubber band if it is too long and cut the excess off. Make sure the matchstick at the end of the candle is even with the edge of the cotton reel, and the matchstick at the other end is longer and sits on the ground.

Hold the tractor in your hand and wind the longer matchstick round and round until it is tight, then put her down on the ground. Your tractor should move along as the matchstick unwinds.

You could even paint your tractor and have races with your friends. You'll have endless hours of fun with this toy and it's sure to get the old man off those bloody computer games.

There are two things in this world that man cannot live without: women and fish. For me, attracting a fish to a fly is like catching a good woman. When fishing, you dress the hook with a mixture of hair, feathers and tinsels to make it attractive to the fish, not unlike when you put on your best suit and tie for a date with a bloody gorgeous woman.

Fishing Tips

Wonder at the beauty of the great outdoors. Savour the aroma of fresh mountain air and moss-covered rocks, like you would the lingering smell of perfume as a woman passes you by.

Marvel at the anticipation of the catch. You might have to cast all day but persevere, because that fish could strike at any time. Like you might have to go down to the pub 150 times before your lady finally walks through that door.

Be thrilled by the strike, the splashy rise of a trout as it takes your fancy fly, the same way a woman finds your looks and your manliness irresistible.

Enjoy the challenge of a fish on your line. Play it like you would a lovely lady's glance across a crowded room. Reel it in slowly, softly, allowing it time to want to finally rest in your arms.

Origin:	Ken Moller of Wairarapa
Hook:	4 to 6
Tail:	Black squirrel
Body:	Dark pink glitter chenille
Hackle:	Pink saddle hackle
Wing:	Pink quill feather
Head:	Dark pink or black

This is my favourite fly. It's my own design and combines the 'Fuzzy Wuzzy Wet Fly' and the 'Winged Dry Fly' styles to create the 'Moist Fly'.

Fly Tying Instructions:
1. Bind the hook shank with thread halfway up ending at the bend.
2. Tie in a bunch of squirrel to create the tail.
3. Tie in a length of pink chenille finishing halfway up the shank. Red or green is the traditional colour for a 'Fuzzy Wuzzy' and some men find it hard to even buy pink. But trust me boys, this little fly will have them jumping out of the water.
4. Now tie in a beautiful set of pink wings.
5. Tie in a hackle of pink.
6. Build up a small head, whip finish and varnish.

Watercress Stuffed Trout
Mix 50 g of cottage cheese with a bunch of roughly chopped watercress.
Add 1tsp of wasabi and 1tbsp of beaten egg. Season with salt and pepper.
Stuff into boned trout. Bake in a covered non-stick pan over a fire beside the river.
Serve with puha and a dark beer.

Going bush is a great Moller tradition. My great-grandfather, Willy Moller, spent most of his life out in the wild, clearing kauri the size of houses with a bullock team, to help carve this country into what it is today. Wally, my Dad, was a Government deer culler and would take me with him every weekend. It was a great time for a young boy. Always, after about four or five hours of hunting Dad would say, 'We'll stop here, boy.' I'd rush off and gather some dry twigs for Dad to boil up the billy and I'd watch as the old man pulled a log up to the fire. He'd sit down and very slowly, he'd pull out his old leather

Me and Ken up the Ureweras

tobacco pouch, place it beside him and begin to roll a ciggie with just one hand. He'd flip open the pouch with his thumb, then with the first two fingers of the same hand he'd pluck from the pouch a cigarette paper and let it flutter into his open palm. Then, with his thumb and forefinger he would tease out just enough tobacco and rub it once or twice between his thumb and first three fingers and then let the tobacco drop gently into the paper sitting in the curve of his palm. Then came the roll – a gentle squeezing of the whole hand, and then he would work the cigarette to the tips of his fingers and out it would pop with the sticky part of the paper right there. A quick lick and a final roll and there she was, the most beautiful one-handed rollie you'd ever laid eyes on. As soon as we had our billy tea in our tin mugs, Dad would tell me stories about great men of the bush and of stags standing 10-foot at the shoulder, and I would hang on every word, marvelling at the unconcerned way in which Dad would light up that one-handed masterpiece. It was like burning the Mona Lisa to me, and to this very day I've never been able to light my own cigarette.

Gidday there folks. Spending a day down on the farm is like spending a day in Mother Nature's classroom. This quiz is for all you city slickers to see if you'd make it as a great New Zealand farmer. Check your answers on page 126.

1. What time of year would you put the bull to the cow?

2. Name two breeds of working sheepdog.

3. What is an anvil used for?

4. What type of farmer would I be if I had Berkshires?

5. If you were using a 'hand-piece', what would you be doing?

6. What is the term farmers use when putting the ram to the ewes?

7. What is a 'sirsingle' used for?

8. What is a 'separator' used for in dairying?

9. How do pigs sweat?

10. Two different animals have the same breed name and produce a type of wool. Name the breed and what type of animals they are.

71

It was on a broad, bright moonlit night, hundreds of years ago that the legendary Willy Moller united the clans of Scotland forever ...

Willy Moller
Willy my great-grandfather

Billy Moller
It was Billy Moller, Willy's only son, who led the clans into battle. He was a fearless warrior and his very name bought fear and loathing to the English.

Robert the Bruce
Bruce pledges his allegiance to Billy Moller, the man who saved Scotland

Big Heart: Grandfather's Love.
The English Princess who helped Billy Moller
and who fell deeply in love with this rogue
of Scotland. She was also renowned for her
triple butter shortbread.

Ken Moller
That's me in my family Tartan carrying on the
tradition of the brave and handsome Moller Clan.

Kenneth Moller
Kenneth, my cousin, and champion
of the Scottish Highland Games,
holder of the National Tosser Title.

There is nothing I love more than to be outside on a wild and stormy night, checking my flock for newborn lambs and making sure they bond with their mothers. But once I'm home, I love to pull up the rocker in front of the fire, usually with a lamb or two who has lost its Mum tucked into a basket and pull out my book of 'Brain Stumpers for Wild and Stormy Nights'. I have created this brain stumper in honour of Camp Mother.

Use the clues to find 41 words and four phrases. Words are written in all directions: forwards, backwards, up, down and diagonal. Once you've found a word, highlight it. The 10 letters left over spell Ken's secret message.

Answers on page 126

```
B L O O D Y G O R G E O U S
A T E A O A A R A E L P K E
C A M P G I D A Y L I G H T
H P O I L L G T O T G R E D
E H T N A Y E U F R I E N D
L A H K E D T A S A B A H A
O N E E P O S T U T L S O C
R I R A P P U B N S E E U T
D T D S A H O R S E R O S E
A E A E X I O N H B O R E A
E I L K E L K R I O A D D R
L O A N S E R O N S S R A C
L B E S T M A T E S T N I A
```

1. Ken's favourite description of Camp Mother (phrase) (14)
2. ---- Mother (4)
3. Common greeting (5)
4. D------- saving (8)
5. Opposite of foe (6)
6. To mail (4)
7. Four-legged animal with mane (5)
8. Ken's favourite flower (4)
9. Dull (4)
10. What farmers need from the bank (5)
11. What Ken does in bed (6)
12. Needed to propel a dinghy (4)
13. Ken and Ken's relationship (phrase) (9)
14. To star in the l--- r--- (8)
15. A rock with mineral components too fine to be seen (8)
16. Camp ------ (6)
17. ---- of cows (4)
18. The colour of Camp Mother's jumpsuit (4)
19. Lack of difficulty in achieving something (4)
20. Camp Mother's allure (phrase) (9)
21. Small devices that perform or aid simple tasks (7)
22. Starchy island food (4)
23. Pulled or stretched tightly (4)
24. Little r-- of s------- (phrase) (13)
25. Money you give out on Hanukkah (4)
26. Sharp sour taste (4)
27. Someone who is in charge of others in a work situation (4)
28. Ken is a most ------- bachelor (8)
29. Ken's favourite Sunday dinner (5)
30. What Ken puts on his hair and his tractor (6)
31. Where Ken's chooks live (8)
32. Maori name for New Zealand (8)
33. Pointed projections on the head of Ken's prize bull (5)
34. Word to refer to a father (3)
35. Body of water surrounded by land where Ken goes fishing (4)
36. Game, --- and match (3)
37. Colour you should never wear around a bull (3)
38. You'll find Ken down at the --- on a Friday night (3)
39. To look at Camp Mother using your eyes (3)
40. Kind or sort (3)
41. A large member of the deer family (3)
42. Mix in an ingredient (3)
43. Man's best friend (3)
44. The first drink Ken has in the morning (3)
45. Ken is the most eligible -------- (8)

Name
Prue Ramsbottom

Born
Hawke's Bay

Educated
Remuera Private Boarding School for Girls

Favourite food
Champagne

Favourite song
'Hey Big Spender'

Most like to meet
Don't be silly darling most people are dying to meet me

Achievements
New Zealand's most elegant smoker and drinker

Desires
To carry on the great Ramsbottom family tradition of smoking and drinking

School for me was such a bore. There was no smoking or drinking.
My favourite childhood memory was bouncing down the runway of the
Serengeti aboard Mummy and Daddy's little fixed-wing plane, scattering
the pretty gazelles, and seeing the little black faces of the children running
to meet our family. Dilly, of course, hated Africa; she abhorred the dust
and the heat. I can still see her puffy red face all covered in Calamine spots
where she had been bitten by the tsetse fly. Jolly rotten luck really.
Mummy had one of our African guides carry Dilly around so she would not
miss out on the shooting expeditions.
I shall always remember my childhood friend Zimbulu, who taught me how
to make a water carrier from the stretched stomach lining of a wildebeest,
it was terribly handy for mixing our drinks.
Late in the afternoon, with gin and tonic in hand, I would watch the lions throw
themselves down in the dusty shade as the sun set over my beloved Africa.
These were the happiest days of my childhood.

Name
Dilly Ramsbottom

Born
Hawke's Bay

Educated
Remuera Private Boarding School for Girls

Favourite food
Lobster and Adriatic salmon in a demiglaze of black caviar and dried figs. Followed by a fricassee of wild pheasant with aubergine, chestnuts and truffles baked in a pig's bladder and served with anchovy butter. Accompanied by a bottle of Dom Perignon and finished off with sweet creamed melon balls filled with raspberries and strawberries soaked in Jamaican rum.

Favourite song
'Da Da Da'

Most like to meet
I've met everyone, darling.

Achievements
Captain of the school tennis and debating teams, although I never participated in either

Desires
To back the Rolls through the main gates without taking off both mirrors

I was a happy, chubby child. I loved boarding school — Prue and I had our own rooms and our ponies boarded there with us. Mummy and Daddy would come by on the weekends and watch us ride. I adored my time there, though I did miss Mummy's parties and all the lovely finger food. I looked forward to the summer break, when we would holiday abroad. Prue loved our little trips to Africa, but my favourite place was the Mediterranean. I would lie on the chaise longue on Daddy's' yacht and get the servants to bring me trays of delicious little morsels and drinks decorated with little tropical orchids that Mummy had flown in daily from Singapore. The Royal Family would holiday with us sometimes. The young princesses, Prue and I would have such lovely parties on the boat and invite all our rich little friends. Gosh, it was all such terribly good fun.

Fah fah fah.

Chukkas darlings

Hello darlings.

I have always thought of myself as a writer. Dilly and I do know a lot of people in the art and literature world. And we are, of course, the patrons of the Filthy Rich Bastards Supporting Struggling Artists, and often hold little soirées and invite some of the more alternative writers.

So it is with great pleasure that I put pen to fine linen paper and set down prose for you pertaining to one of our greatest passions: Champagne Polo.

Champagne Polo is quite different from the traditional game, because in the champagne version you're not really aware of the men on horseback with mallets in hand. The match is simply on in the background, and what a fabulously gorgeous backdrop it is to a day of socialising and drinking.

The thwack of the mallet on the ball and the smell of freshly cut grass create the perfect atmosphere for the popping of another bottle of champers.

Charles and Lady Camilla, both very, very dear friends of ours, often join us at the back of the Roller for a snort or two after the Prince has played a few chukkas on one of their many visits to us over the summer holiday season.

Just as polo players must abide by the rules of their little game, there are some things you need to know in order to get the most pleasure out of Champagne Polo.

There are six chukkas in a game, each lasting approximately seven minutes. So you've got time to pop around to the bar in the boot of the Rolls and top up at least 14 to 15 times during a match. In the high society horsy world, when toasting one's glass, it is appropriate to say, 'chukkas' rather than, 'cheers'. It is derived from the Indian word 'chukka', which, loosely translated, means jolly good luck on the polo field, and does not hail from the time Dilly was throwing up behind the Rolls on a particularly hot day after 25 bottles of champagne, as some of the common people have mistakenly assumed.

Our favourite moment of Champagne Polo is halftime when, on the completion of the third chukka, all the players and ponies have a little rest. The public is asked to go out onto the field and replace the divots the little ponies have turned up. This is a golden opportunity for the common people to rub shoulders with the likes of ourselves and, although we rarely speak with them, it's a time when they can linger for a brief moment with a higher class of people.

Of course, Dilly and I do end up bringing most of the divots back with us, as high heels have a tendency to pick up the divots rather than pat them down. But it is all in good fun and gives us a sense of mucking in.

All in all it's a great day out, this wonderful Sport of Kings. See you all at the Saville Cup. Chukkas, darlings.

Camp Mother victorious at polo tournament

Across

1. The thing Prue and Dilly belong to that's high.
4. Something very private for rich people.
6. Used to indicate position.
7. Pertaining to heat.
9. Used to indicate location.
10. Prue and Dilly have many of these dwellings.
12. To continue supplying alcohol (in Prue and Dillys case).
13. Prue and Dilly have a Persian one.
15. Prue and Dilly are what you call living replicas of these.
16. A form of 'a' used before words beginning with a vowel.
18. Something worth a lot when Prue and Dilly write it out.
19. Means nickel (shortened).
22. The only drink for Prue and Dilly.
27. The act of weeping.
29. Prue and Dilly tip with this.
32. To lose interest.
33. Prue and Dilly order this to come round the front.
34. Conclusion.
35. Something you win in tennis.
37. Describing hen's teeth.
40. Something Prue and Dilly would never do with their own bags.
41. Yields from Prue and Dilly's investments.
43. How Prue and Dilly would describe Raelene and Brenda.
44. A word our wealthy duo never hear.
45. An old drink.
47. The best or ultimate in something.
48. Shackles.
50. A place to bake, but not a cake.
51. Where Prue and Dilly party when holidaying in London.

Down

2. One that is adored.
3. Prue and Dilly have six of these moored.
5. Prue and Dilly shake a martini, but would have their chef do this to a salad.
7. Something you'd put a feather into.
8. One of the oceans crossed by Prue and Dilly.
11. Filthy rich.
13. A big wig in the army.
14. How you should reply to an invitation to one of Prue and Dilly's parties.
15. Animals of a region.
20. Something that means everything to Prue and Dilly.
21. Dilly's plumpness.
23. Something both socialites may have if they don't stop drinking.
24. To bring or take.
25. To deviate from the proper course.
26. In the habit of.
28. Something our tipsy old gals don't get much of these days.
30. Expressive of surprise.
31. To extend hospitality.
36. Something that happens to all good silve
38. Both Prue and Dilly are directors of this (abbr).
39. To ascertain the mood.
42. In no way.
46. What Prue and Dilly will be sending ou when the booze has run out.
49. Something the gals would never say when offered another drink.

Check your answers on page 126.

One of the most exciting things one can do is to stand in the owners' box and urge on one's favourite racehorse, as she takes out the big race.

The Ramsbottoms have owned racehorses for centuries and Dilly and I, of course, continue this great tradition. We have owned many racehorses over the years but purchased our favourite, a big leggy chestnut, just last year at the national yearling sales. We had to outbid Sheikh Mohammed and that wily little Irish breeder from County Cork, but ended up getting her for a song and a dance really. Dilly names all the little racing ponies and she's called this one, Big Leggy Chestnut.

Dilly loves to go down and lead our horses in after they've won their races, and I do love to watch. Darling Dilly has no idea when it comes to horses but as an owner, she likes to share in its glory after winning the big race. Just last week we were at Ellerslie and Big Leggy Chestnut was racing in the fifth. Dilly went down to lead her in after she won and, as soon as the groom handed Dilly the rope, Big Leggy Chestnut ran right over the top of Dill, flattening her directly in front of the VIP stand. She lost one of her new shoes and her hat went flying into the common area and caused a crush of people up against the fence as they rushed to see what was happening. This commotion frightened the little pony that had run second and it reared up and sent its jockey flying into the rose bushes. As Dilly stood up and dusted herself off, Big Leggy Chestnut rubbed her sweaty face all over her and the bridle got caught on the epaulette of Dill's new jacket which caused her to be promptly lifted off the ground and swung around like a ragdoll. Of course Dilly's screaming didn't help and before you knew it, poor old Big Leggy Chestnut bolted back out onto the track. She did a lovely lap of honour with Dilly flapping about before the grooms finally caught up with them and unhooked poor old Dilly. Eventually everyone reassembled around the trophy table and all was well once again; jockeys smiled, cameras flashed and Dilly waved out to me – holding up the cup and looking like she had been dragged backwards through a compost heap.

I, of course, picked up the cheque, had the grooms deliver Dilly to the car, and marvelled at the fun we all have at such occasions. There really is nothing quite like a day at the races.

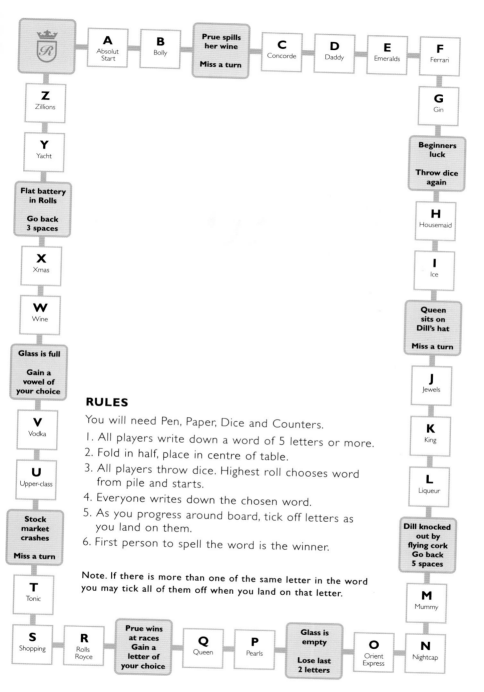

A Absolut Start

B Bolly

Prue spills her wine — Miss a turn

C Concorde

D Daddy

E Emeralds

F Ferrari

G Gin

Beginners luck — Throw dice again

H Housemaid

I Ice

Queen sits on Dill's hat — Miss a turn

J Jewels

K King

L Liqueur

Dill knocked out by flying cork Go back 5 spaces

M Mummy

N Nightcap

O Orient Express

Glass is empty — Lose last 2 letters

P Pearls

Q Queen

Prue wins at races Gain a letter of your choice

R Rolls Royce

S Shopping

T Tonic

Stock market crashes — Miss a turn

U Upper-class

V Vodka

Glass is full Gain a vowel of your choice

W Wine

X Xmas

Flat battery in Rolls Go back 3 spaces

Y Yacht

Z Zillions

RULES

You will need Pen, Paper, Dice and Counters.

1. All players write down a word of 5 letters or more.
2. Fold in half, place in centre of table.
3. All players throw dice. Highest roll chooses word from pile and starts.
4. Everyone writes down the chosen word.
5. As you progress around board, tick off letters as you land on them.
6. First person to spell the word is the winner.

Note. If there is more than one of the same letter in the word you may tick all of them off when you land on that letter.

Prue And Dilly's Chairman Of The Board Game

Prue And Dilly's Chairman Of The Board Game

85

Every year Prue and I attend the Davidson's hunt. Although Prue is never good in the morning she is happy to rise early on hunt day, lured by the Hot Buttered Rum which is traditionally taken by the riders and spectators as a warming tonic, while the horses snort and stamp their hooves in anticipation of the run.
We find there is nothing more invigorating than sipping on this drink while being driven behind the horses and hounds in the Land Rover.

Hot Buttered Rum
Place in a hot tall glass:
1 tspn powdered sugar
1/4 cup boiling water
1/4 cup rum
Add 1 tbsp butter
Top up glass with boiling water
Sprinkle with freshly grated nutmeg.

Dilly and I usually quench our thirst with this next drink at lunchtime, while parked on a hill overlooking the riders and hounds.

Champagne A La Natural
Open a very large bottle of Dom
Pour into a very expensive champagne flute
Drink until finished.

Chef is also giving you the recipe for our favourite afternoon snack, Sherried Chicken Bits. The little toothpicks make them terribly convenient when eating and drinking while being driven over rough terrain.

Sherried Chicken Bits
The breasts of two fat stewing hens
Good sherry

Stew breasts and while still warm place into a large jar
Cover with sherry
Seal jar and refrigerate for 10 days
To serve, skin, bone and cut meat into bite-size portions
Place on toothpicks and serve with an aged port.

Lorna and I both lost our husbands 10 years ago. Reg and Dick were cremated on the same day and we met at the crematorium. We took up bowls the day after Reg and Dick's funerals. We had so much fun that we now spend our weekends travelling to bowling tournaments throughout New Zealand.

We are both keen gardeners and love to collect cuttings for our little gardens when we travel from bowling club to bowling club. While winning a tournament is always very satisfying, you just can't beat the feeling of rooting something that you've found on your journey. When taking a cutting, a good size is needed if you want a good root, and if you keep it wet and rolled up in newspaper it can last for days.

Once you've got your specimen home, pop it in a jar of water and allow the root hairs to develop. When you've got a good root system plant it out in the garden and watch it blossom. Just last week we scattered Reg and Dick's ashes over a lovely specimen we had just rooted in the garden.

This year, Lorna and I have decided to drive to the national bowling championships and to stop off at all the bowling clubs along the way. Of course, we will collect cuttings wherever we can. Lorna has packed her secateurs and her loppers (for the bigger specimens) and we have even modified the Morris Minor so we can now root in the boot.

Lorna and I have been rooting for years, it's a great hobby and we reckon it keeps us young.

It couldn't have been any more than 10 o'clock – big hand was on the 12, little hand was on the nine. Gillian, my partner, was thumbing through a dog-eared file on two dames. The Topp Twins were known to everyone in my business as the 'Metamorphous Madams'. My job was to track them down. They ran a seedy nightclub down on the east side, near the meat market. But I could see right through them. It was a front for something and I was determined to find out just what they were up to. I'd never been able to pin them down – they were always one costume change ahead of me. One minute they were street girls who went by the names Raelene and Brenda. Then, with a flick of a cardy, they'd turn themselves into two melt-in-your-mouth dames, Camp Mother and Camp Leader. The next minute they'd be leaning on a bar, beer in hand, and heading to the little boys' room. They had

espionage written all over them and on the toilet walls as well. If I thought of my job as a potent alcoholic cocktail, these broads were a double whammy Harvey Wallbanger with a liqueur cherry on top. It was as clear as mud. But private dicks don't lie down when the bus is coming, oh no, they hail that bus and ride it all the way to the liquor store.

Outside the streetlights were sending off a hazy glow as I pulled my coat around me and left the office. 'Goodnight, Susan,' said Gillian.

I was doing the late-shift and somewhere out there was a whiskey sour and the sweet smell of success. All I needed was a lucky break. I stood in the doorway of a cheap hotel and lit my last cigarette. Well, it wasn't my last, but my packet would be empty once I smoked it, if you get my drift. It started to rain. I was torn between heading home to an empty apartment or Maize Simpson's strip joint down on the east side. I kicked at an empty bottle in the alleyway and turned left at the end. That's when I saw it. A neon sign flashed 'Girly Bar' and the outline of a naked woman winked at me. The Metamorphous Madams notorious women's club, frequented by dames who wore men's shoes and lipstick blondes in double-breasted jackets.

Suddenly the hair on my back stood up (I hadn't shaved lately) and I felt like I was being watched. I ducked into the entrance of the club. Suddenly Gillian appeared – she seemed startled as I stepped out of the shadows. 'Susan,' she said, 'What are you doing here? This is the notorious women's club.' I looked down. I had two breasts and a great set of legs. Sure I could get in, but what ran though my mind as we climbed the stairs was, what was Gillian doing here?

I ordered a whiskey on the rocks. The joint was full of dames. Two gorgeous blondes peered at me over the tops of their martinis, and two others straight out of a gangster movie leaned on the pool table and gave me 'that look'. The blondes were with them. I didn't want any trouble so I looked around for Gillian. I caught a glimpse of her though a shaft of smoky light on the dance floor. And then it hit me like a runaway truck! Side on she looked a lot like Camp Leader!

Had one of the Metamorphous Madams been posing as my partner Gillian? Holy Toledo. One of the Topp Twins had been right under my nose the whole time. I slipped out through the back way, down the fire escape before Gillian – or was it Camp Leader, or Raelene, or Ken could see that I had recognised her, or was it him.

It was still raining as I stepped out on to the street and turned up the collar of my coat. All I had to do now was to find the other sister. I reached for my cigarettes and remembered that I was all out of fags. I knew a joint on 5th where you could get a drink and a cigarette late at night, and I turned and disappeared into the darkness . . .

Name
Belle Gingham

Born
In The hay barn

School
No formal education

Favourite food
16 oz steak

Favourite song
'Stand By Your Man'

Most like to meet
Dolly Parton

Achievements
Winner; Taihape Young Country Entertainer 1968

Desires
To play at The 'Grand Ole Oprey'

When I was little I wanted my own puppy but Mama and
Papa couldn'T afford one so my sister Belle and me, we had
ourselves a pet hedgehog. We called him Prickles and when we
sang around The campfire aT night, he'd come out and sit with
us and listen To our songs. Whenever Belle yodelled, he'd curl up
into a ball and fall asleep by The fire. He wasn't allowed up on
my bunk in case he fell on Belle and sTabbed her in The nighT.
Belle and me sTuffed Prickles afTer he died of mulTiple disease.
Today, he has pride of place on The manTlepiece.

Name
Belle Gingham

Born
Halfway between the hay barn and the cowshed

Educated
Never went to school, but learnt everything a girl needs to know down on the farm.

Favourite food
Rabbit stew

Favourite song
'Going To Be a Country Gal Again'

Most like to meet
Minnie Pearl

Achievements
Champion Spoon Player of New Zealand for 21 years running

Desires
To get new elastic in the waist of my gingham skirt

When we were born, Mama and Papa were so poor that Mama had to cut up her favourite gingham tablecloth so we kids could have nappies. We loved those nappies so much that we got our Mama to make us gingham skirts and we've been wearing them ever since. My sister Belle and me, we grew up on the farm. We sure love being country folk. Back when Mama and Papa and Prickles were alive, we'd all sit around the fire after a big plate of possum stew. Prickles our pet hedgehog would drink homebrew from a saucer. Mama would get out her fiddle, Papa played the tea-chest bass, Belle strummed the old guitar, and I would play the spoons and yodel. It was pure heaven.

Belle and me were driving in the country one fine day,
It was in the heat of summer and Dad was making hay.
We were on the tractor, a Fergie painted red,
Loading up the bales and putting them in the shed.
As we crossed the paddock for another bale or two,
The bull jumped over the fence and came into our view.
He was heading for our tractor, drawn by the colour red.
Belle took one look at me and yelled, 'We're flippin dead.'
I started weaving that old Fergie back and forward and back,
But the bull was gaining on us like a racehorse on the track.
We went flying through the fence and Belle yelled,
      'Head her for the dam!'
But now we had another worry – being bunted by the ram.
We headed for the pigsty, beside a row of trees.
We thought we'd find some safety there but hit a swarm of bees.
Things were getting messy as we swerved to miss the sows.
We sideswiped the henhouse and were heading for the cows.
Well you wouldn't read about it, that was our saving grace.
The old bull loved those Jerseys and he gave up on the chase.
He was lovestruck, that's what saved our lives.
Then Dad scooped up the bees and took them to his hives.
It was just another day, down home on the farm.
Okay, it was dangerous, but no one came to harm.
And from that day onwards, Dad paints his tractors black,
Belle and me became big country stars,
And we drive a Cadillac.

Back in 1956 our great-grandmother, Phrilly Gingham, ran the Greasy Spoon Tearooms on the outskirts of Ohinewai. She was famous for her cooking but she was also the greatest spoon player this land has ever seen. She could play any kind of spoon: soup spoon, teaspoon, tablespoon, dessertspoon, she even played the ladle. Sometimes she'd roll them spoons around her body and everyone would hoot and holler.

Truckers from far and wide would pull into the Greasy Spoon Tearooms to eat their steak and eggs and watch Phrilly do a little number. Belle would go to the Greasy Spoon Tearooms each summer holiday to help Grandma Phrilly, but mostly she would just gawk at Grandma and the way she handled that silverware.

It was a sad day when Grandma passed away. All the truckers made a cavalcade as a guard of honour that went from Pukekohe to Ngaruawahia and everyone who came to wish Grandma a fond farewell brought a set of spoons and played 'Now Is The Hour'. It was real moving and at the wake everyone swapped spoons with each other and that's how spoon collecting became such a big thing in New Zealand.

Now Belle is carrying on the family's spoon-playing tradition and people say she's just as good as Grandma Phrilly.

Phrilly Gingham 1878–1978

How To Play The Spoons:

Place a dessertspoon between your index finger and middle finger and a soup spoon between your index finger and thumb. Make sure the spoons are placed back to back and hold them together firmly. Bang the spoons on your leg until you get a steady tap happening.

For variations of sound, bang spoons on your leg and then as you come up, bang the soup spoon on the underside of your other hand.

You can also spread the fingers of your free hand, hold them rigid and drag the spoons down fingers to get a rat-a-tat-tat sound.

Put a country song on the wind-up and play along.

Belle and me have written a song to test your knowledge of country music. Each verse contains a clue in bold that will make you think of the title of a famous country song. Guess the title of the song and check your answers on page 126. Guess all nine songs correctly and win a no-expenses paid trip to Nashville.

Country music is our passion, we sing songs about real life
Rockin' chairs, love affairs
And the parting ways of man and wife

It's always really meaningful, a story's always told
Woven with a shiny thread
Which will sew the seeds of gold

Songs for every lover, the drifter and the liar
There's always something out there
That will fuel your song of fire

The burning desert holds no watery gift, the rider's biggest fear
But water's not the only drink you cannot find round here

There are horses on the gallop and cowboys free to roam
But deep down they're always searching
For the colour of their home

They carry with them memories of that nearly fateful day
When the poker game turned nasty
And they turned and walked away

And even then they had one hand upon their gun
All seven of them praying to the altar of the sun

So cowboys often end up riding fast or lying dead
If only they had listened to what old Willie said

But there will never be a day when country music dies
Though you might leave me once again
I'll wipe the teardrops from my eyes

Belle and me, we love to go hunting for rabbit. And when we catch us one, we cook up a rabbit stew. Mama always said you have to have three veggies with any kind of meat. So, here's our recipe for 'Rabbit Stew with Mashed Spuds', 'Corn Grilled in Husks' and 'Faggot of Beans'.

Rabbit Stew
1 rabbit
Salt and pepper
3 onions
2 oz butter
1 tbsp flour
1 pint beer
Fresh herbs
1 tspn mustard
Bacon

Soak your rabbit in cold salted water for 1 hour. Dry well. Cut into joints and sprinkle with salt and pepper. Melt 1 oz of butter in a frying pan. Add onion and bacon and fry until cooked. Add remaining butter and fry rabbit until golden-brown. Stir in flour and blend well. Add beer and stir well. Transfer ingredients from frying pan into casserole dish. Add sugar, herbs and mustard. Bake in a coal range (350° F) for about 2 hours.

Mashed Spuds
Bag of spuds
Butter
Peel spuds. Boil. Mash. Add butter.

Corn Grilled in Husks
Strip outer husks off corn. Grill over glowing coals.

Faggot of Beans
Cut ends off green beans and remove strings. Tie 8–10 beans in bundles with spring onions. One bundle is one serving. Bring to the boil 1 cup of water and 1 oz butter. Lower heat and cook beans for 15 minutes until tender.

Serve on a tin plate.

Don't forget to eat all your veggies and have a sing-along around the fire after dinner.

Name
Jools Topp

Born
Huntly Maternity, 14 May 1958
at 10.05pm

School
Gordonton School, Ruawaro School
and Huntly College

Favourite Food
Mary's Mexican Tacos

Favourite Song
'Infamous Angel' by Iris DeMent

Qualifications
School C, Best Performance in an Entertainment Programme,
Best Entertainers, Best Country Album, Level 1 Natural
Horsemanship

Desires
To keep on singing and be a great horsewoman

Since we started performing, it has been a roller coaster ride of fun
and laughter. Lynda and I have travelled halfway around the world
entertaining folks with our kiwi style of humour. I love the places
we've been and the people we've met, and still love setting off on a
tour of New Zealand, or playing the Tamworth Country Music
Festival in Australia or the Michigan Womyn's Music Festival in
America. But, to me, New Zealand will always be home, and there's
nothing I enjoy more than getting back to the farm to ride my
horse on the wild west coast.

The Topp Twins

106

Name
Lynda Topp

Born
Huntly Maternity, 14 May 1958
at 10.10pm

Educated
Gordonton School, Ruawaro School,
Huntly College. Excelled in Sport

Favourite Food
Sushi

Favourite Song
'My Pinto Pony and I'

Achievements
School Cert, Best Performance in an Entertainment Programme,
Best Entertainers, Best Country Music Album, Best International
Comedy Duo and International Swiss Yodelling Champion at the Old
Time Country Music Festival, USA.

Desires
To be one of the great yodellers in the world.

Ever since I was little, I believed Jools and I would save the world.
We've got a little more work to do on the world, but I do believe we
have changed people's attitudes. Through our music and comedy, we
have helped New Zealand become nuclear free, supported Maori land
rights, and spoken out for the Gay and Lesbian community. Making
New Zealanders laugh about themselves and the things that affect
them has been a great way to get our message across, and the
positive response from people in this country has made us proud
to be Kiwi gals.

Well, you have finally reached the real characters; Lynda and myself. I guess you could say that we are just as mad as the characters we play. We do like to have a lot of fun, and we have managed to do just that in our 25 years as entertainers.

Over the years, we have developed a style of performance that is our very own and during numerous trips overseas we have realised there is no one else like us anywhere in the world.

We both believe that coming from New Zealand has helped us establish our unique sense of humour and allowed us to incorporate the theatrical side of entertainment into our shows.

We are real Kiwis through and through and we wouldn't live anywhere else in the world.

One of our favourite things to do is to pack up the caravan and head out on tour. Every moment on the road is an adventure. We've done a few miles over the years and have more than a few good stories to tell from our experiences from our time on the road.

Way back in the late 70s we were driving back from Punakaiki along the West Coast and a bunch of cool-looking hippies driving an old truck with three dogs on the back were in front of us.

As we drove, we could see them passing a big old joint back and forth to each other just getting high on the beautiful day and trucking along. However, they went round a pretty sharp corner and one of the dogs, a little fox terrier, came off the back of the truck. We immediately sprang into action and raced our car up to the back of the truck to try and let them know about the little fella running for his life after them.

Well, those folks were in la-la land, so all the honking and light-flashing and yelling from us fell on deaf ears. This went on for about five miles and the dog was starting to get tuckered out so we tried to catch him. But he wasn't having a bar of that, so we just kept up the chase. Finally, we noticed that up ahead there was a sharp u-bend in the road, and that if we got close enough, we would be parallel to them. It was our last chance to alert them before the dog keeled over and died.

So just as they turned, we stared yelling our lungs out and we finally got their attention. And at the very same moment, the wee dog took an almighty leap and jumped back up on the truck!

Those hippies just thought we were a mad pair of women, and to this very day, know nothing of the drama that had unfolded behind them. We couldn't help but smile at the outcome of the whole crazy event.

Along the way, on our travels, people have given us free lunches in their tearooms, asked for a million autographs, told us how much they love our telly programmes, bought us many a jug of beer in the pub if we would sing them one song (which of course always turned into about three hours of drinking and partying), and let us into their hearts and supported our shows in their towns.

We are still doing all of this today. In fact, this very weekend the girls at the Whitebait Inn in Mokau cooked us up the biggest and best whitebait fritters in this land and sent us on our way with our money still in our pockets. If anybody asked us to sum up New Zealanders, we think one word says it all: generous.

We have even started up our own International Sheep Rescue (ISR) team. Well, its only me and Lynda who are officially in this organisation, but our job is to find any cast sheep in paddocks and get them back up on their feet. To this day the ISR has saved 57 sheep throughout New Zealand.

We've played in theatres, pubs, woolsheds, local halls, parks, and on the streets. We've marvelled at the breathtaking scenery we have been lucky enough to travel through.

When the leaves are turning gold and red along the road from Arrowtown to Wanaka, or when the lambs are sheltering behind their Mums along the snow-covered lowlands from Mautara to Longbush, or when the hot sun streams through the windows of our vehicle as we drive along the coastal road from Pukehina down to Opotiki on our way to the Gisborne A&P show, these are just some of the great moments we will remember of our touring days.

So, if you pass us on the road pulling our little caravan, chances are there is another big adventure just waiting to happen around the corner.

Our audience at Canterbury A & P Show, 2001

One of our most favourite tours was the Gypsy Caravan Tour in 1989. We found the caravan behind the organic gardens in Grey Lynn. It looked like something out of a picturebook and it was for sale. Gypsy Mike had already sold the horses, so we bought a horseless carriage and figured we'd worry about how to pull it later on. We hired the local tow truck company to haul the caravan to our front yard where she stayed while we rebuilt and refurbished her. We found the pulling power on a trip down south in the form of a beautiful old tractor. Six months later, we hooked the tractor up and hit the road for for 91 days. We kept a daily journal of our tour and below is our first entry.

10.1.89
Pull out of Auckland 5.25 am. We have not alerted authorities about driving a tractor across the Harbour Bridge. 5.35 am, flashing lights surround us. Cheery traffic cops escort us across the bridge, wave goodbye and wish us good luck.

Off the bridge by 5.50am. Turn off at Akaranga Drive and go up Highway 27. Arrive Albany 6.30 am. Stop off in Kaukaupakaupa at 7.00 am for diesel, oil and a cuppa. Back on the road at 7.35 am.

Pass through Silverdale at 7.49 am. Sports car tailing us for 15 minutes. Just outside Silverdale, sports car pulls us over. It's a newspaperman from the Rodney Times. Wants a photo with us. Arrange to meet at Puhoi at 3 pm. We cruise into Orewa at 8 am, four hours ahead of schedule. Park the tractor and caravan by the beach and put the billy on for morning tea. A woman from the local paper calls in swearing like a trooper. Isn't swearing about anything in particular, it is just part of her vocab. We chat to her about the tour then she waves goodbye and drives off yelling out, 'Have a good time you lucky buggers, have a bloody good tour.' Ziggy pulls up in his housetruck to say hi and has a cuppa with us before heading off up north.

Just finish the dishes and are having a bit of a rest when car pulls up. It's the bloke from the arts and crafts shop Zanadu that's down the road. Says Balinese imports are discounted by 20% for the Topp Twins, if we want to swing by the shop. Nice of him to offer but we don't know whether it is our style.

It's 11.48 am and the Hare Krishnas drop off a fresh garland of flowers and their latest Hare book. The president of the Orewa Lions Club calls in to say gidday and we pose with a family from Stratford and sign autographs at 12 pm.

The gypsy caravan is creating a stir and the rig looks pretty beautiful parked under the trees with the sea in the background.

We pull out at 1.30 pm and arrive at the Puhoi Pub at 2.35 pm. We have invited 200 people to join us at the Puhoi Domain for a barbecue followed by a performance at the local hall to launch the tour. We have asked for koha on the door.

Barbie starts at around 5.30 and more than 200 people hoe into sausages and beers and lap up the late afternoon sun. Tractor rides for the kids and guided tours of the caravan for everyone.

Show starts at 7.30 pm, 500 people cram into the cutest hall this side of the black stump. Show goes like clockwork until a local possum climbs the power pole outside the hall and causes powercut to the whole district. We unhook the tractor and drive her through the main doors to light the stage with her headlights and finish the show around 10.00 pm.

Our audience heads off into the dark but leaves us with $4000 in koha, enough to pay our crew for the next week and get us through the next few gigs.

A great start to the Great New Zealand Gypsy Caravan Tour!

After touring New Zealand, we needed to find out if we could make it internationally. We did, and now we spend three to four months a year performing overseas.

We've played the Edinburgh Fringe Festival, the music and comedy festivals in Montreal, Vancouver and Winipeg and various pubs in Dublin and Cork. We've done theatre seasons in London and here we are wowing the Aussies at the Woman 150 Celebrations in Melbourne.

The dictionary defines the word gay as happy. We are happy. We are gay. And we are happy to be gay. In fact, being openly gay has become a responsibility for us.

Throughout our career, people have thanked us for our visibility as lesbians. They've come up to us after shows to tell us we're positive role models for them, that we've given them the strength to come out and that we've helped make being gay into something to celebrate.

A young gay man wrote us a beautiful letter telling us how much he and his family loved the Topp Twins TV series, and how he decided the show would make a fabulous backdrop for his coming out. As they all sat watching Ken and Ken, and Camp Mother and Camp Leader, he said to his Mum and Dad, 'I'm just like the Topp Twins.' They replied, 'Don't be silly dear, you're not as funny as them!'

To live life as an openly gay or lesbian person, one has to make the decision to come out at some point. It can be a difficult decision to make, and at one time or another, probably scares the living daylights out of everyone who makes it. We worry that people will desert us, that they'll hate us for our choice, that they won't understand.

From our experience, we think the only thing people need to understand about coming out is love: that the parents, family and friends of gay men and lesbian women need to offer their unconditional, non-judgemental love. That it is this kind of love that makes coming out and living an open and fulfilling life easier for everyone.

When we came out, we were lucky to have family and friends who loved us no matter what our decisions in life. And we thank them for that. We also thank our partners for their love and support. And we thank New Zealanders who have always been accepting of our music, humour and sexuality.

Bad lesbian hair day!

I was seven years old when I heard my first yodel. I'd just hopped off my horse outside our neighbours, Wayne and Marilyn, when I heard June Holmes, Australia's yodelling sweetheart, belting out 'My Pinto Pony and I', on the wind-up gramaphone.

Marilyn said my eyes went all funny while I listened to that song. She thought I'd fallen ill, but realised that I'd gone into a yodel coma. When I came to at the end of the song, I declared that one day, I would yodel like June Holmes.

From that day forward, Jools and I would ride up to our neighbours house to listen to the wind-up every chance we got. We'd play 'My Pinto Pony and I' over and over again to get the song firmly fixed in our heads, ride home like the clappers and try to pluck out what we'd heard on our old guitar.

Us with the great Patsy Montana

It wasn't the best way to learn to yodel. Sometimes, we'd forget the song and have to ride back up to the neighbours and race back home a few times a day. But, we finally did get it to sound right. And, as an added consequence of the countless trips back and forth, became very good horse women.

I performed my first yodel in public when I was 17. We were at the Huntly South Rugby Club rooting on our local boys as they played Taniwharau. Huntly South won so we all had a few beers after the match and someone brought out a guitar. After much coaxing I launched into 'My Pinto Pony and I'. Everybody said my yodelling was pretty good and that maybe one day I'd be a big country music star. Jools never learnt to yodel even though she came with me on every trip to hear that old wind-up. But something must have rubbed off on her because she can yodel if she's singing with me. If I stop she sounds like a chook caught in a mincer!

Over the years, yodelling has become an important part of our show and now people expect a yodel whenever the Topp Twins perform.

Oh the confusion of it all. Here Lynda uses Ken Moller's tractor to pull Camp Mother and Camp Leader's little Bambina out of the mud, while I look on.

Developing all the characters has been a really fun part of our career. I'm sure there are people all over New Zealand who have an auntie like Camp Mother or a friend just like Camp Leader. Most folks say they have a neighbour up the road who's the spitting image of Ken Moller, and Brenda and Raelene have clones all over the world.

Strangely enough, none of the characters are based on anyone we know in particular, but more on the types of people you associate with and find in New Zealand culture.

You need only visit the Hawke's Bay to see Prue and Dilly's relations at one of the many wineries, or visit the Papakura Bowling Club to see a hundred Mavis and Lorna's playing in the bowls tournament.

We are often asked why all our characters work so well and the reasons why they have endeared themselves to the Kiwi psyche. Our usual reply is that we have no idea and we are a bit frightened to analyse the whole thing really! Remember the great Kiwi saying, 'if it ain't broke, don't fix it'.

However, one thing we have always consciously instilled in the characters is a positive side. They will all give anything a go, and we think that has endeared them to the public.

Camp Mother says people love her because she has fabulous fashion sense and can mix easily with a variety of people, while Camp Leader carved out her place in the public's heart by always trying too hard and being enthusiastic about everything she does.

Even though we don't like to analyse the whole thing, we think maybe one thing that has allowed our characters to develop, is that they aren't ruled by society's conventions, but do what they know in their hearts is right and fun. We have dared to laugh at ourselves and our country, have been passionate about our career, and brought the rest of the population along for the ride.

She's been a bloody gorgeous ride so far.

We couldn't write a book about the characters without including our four-legged stars. Kelly and Monday were our first show dogs. They travelled with us on the Gypsy Caravan Tour. Kelly guarded the caravan for us and Monday used to come on stage and drink a glass of beer.

River was the next dog to appear on stage with us. She wasn't a flamboyant performer, but she was very focused. She'd stand in one place on stage and stare out at the audience. We'd tell everyone she was our talent scout, searching the theatre for someone she thought looked promising. Really she was just trying to spot our sound operator out there whom she adored.

Phantom, a border collie, was the next big star. Ken Moller would send him out to round up the audience. Sheep dog that he is, herding came naturally, but to get him to herd on cue I'd bounce the lights off my guitar and out into the auditorium and Phantom would chase the spot I created. Border Collies naturally chase a torch light or a reflection so we didn't have to train Phantom at all. Though one day we nearly gave him a heart attack when we turned on a mirror ball at dress rehearsal. Phantom did about 100 kms going after all the tiny reflections before we could turn it off.

River guarding the busking money

The latest and probably most famous dog star in the family is Jack. He's a German Shepherd-Staffie Bull Terrier cross. He sounds ferocious, but he's the gentlest mutt you ever laid eyes on. Jack has a talent we've never seen in another dog. He's a singer and when old Kenny boy plays his harmonica, Jack just can't help but sing along. Jack walks onto the stage by himself, positions himself right in the centre and sings his little heart out on cue every time. Jack performed in every show on our last national tour.

The dogs always steal the show, but we don't mind. They're a constant source of companionship and enjoyment in our lives and on the road.

Phantom is semi-retired now, but Jack is going strong. He's even requested a bigger dressing room for the next tour.

It's just another highway
Just another roadside café
Just another airport
Just another train-stop away
It's just another milestone on a long travelling day

And how does the grass grow on your side of the fence?
And how does the moon shine on your side of the world?

And if I kissed your mouth with mine
Would you say I was out of line?
It's just another time
Just another clock on the wall
It's just another hero who's waiting to fall

And how does the wind blow on your side of the earth?
And how do the clouds fly on your side of the sky?

There's nothing like a party with friends
Up on Highbury fields again
Cause it's just another heartbeat
Just another line to be said
Just another city
Just another place to rest my head
It's just another feeling
And there's no one in my bed

And how does the rain fall on your side of the road?
And how does the sea melt on your side of the snow?

It's just another highway
Just another roadside café
Just another airport
Just another train stop away
It's just another milestone on a long travelling day

On a long travelling day
On a long travelling day

Chorus

**We're untouchable, untouchable, untouchable girls
Untouchable, untouchable, untouchable girls
We're untouchable, untouchable, untouchable girls
We're untouchable, touchable girls.**

Hey we don't let anybody touch our brains
We will never ever plug into the mains
And we are overtaking on a single lane
We're untouchable, touchable girls

Chorus

We live in a world that doesn't care too much
You've got to stand up
You've got to have guts
Yeah we are untouchable but we touch
We're untouchable, touchable girls

Chorus

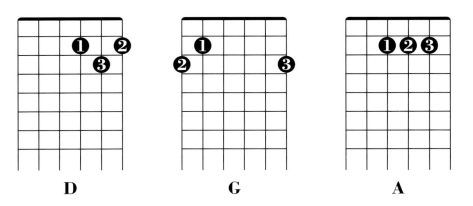

D   G   A

Guitar chords for 'Untouchable Girls'

Mum Topp as the can-can gal in the Ruawaro WDFF Xmas Party.

It's pretty hard to go past Jean Topp's gingernuts, peanut brownies, or louise cake. We think she's the best cook in the world! When we were growing up the cookie jars were always full, but cooking isn't all Mum did. She milked the cows, did all the housework, was the president of the PTA, won first prize for her bearded irises every year and performed at the Women's Division of Federated Farmers annual Christmas show.

Mum taught us to sing. She's got a bit of the performer in her and every now and then we get her up on stage to do a number with us. It's always special when Mum sings 'Spring Time In the Rockies' with us, the very first song she taught us.

Our mum is the kind of mum you want to hug a lot. She falls asleep in front of the telly while she's knitting a new jersey for one of us kids, she steals cuttings just like Mavis and Lorna, still stocks the biscuit jars for our visits and never judges us. She's raised two entertaining lesbians and a gay florist and has always loved us. She is one of a kind, and she's the angel at our table: breakfast, lunch and dinner.

Thanks Mum, we love ya.

When we were little, we used to follow Dad wherever he went. We couldn't wait to put on our little gumboots and help Dad bring in the cows for milking, catch the horses, or feed out the hay in wintertime. Dad taught us that it didn't matter if you were a woman or a bloke, but that if you rolled your sleeves up and worked hard you could do anything.

Dad also taught us to laugh, 'cos Peter Topp is a real joker. We reckon we got our sense of humour from him. Dad'll think up a great one liner and save it for six months or more. Then he'll pop it out when the time is right, and then chuckle to himself about it for weeks.

Dad is also a great horseman and he taught us to ride when we were about six or seven. He told us that you had to fall off your nag at least 10 times before you were a good rider, so Jools and I would ride around the front paddock and throw ourselves off the old horse we were learning on.

Dad has always been there for us and early on taught us everything we needed to know. We were lucky. But we think Dad was pretty lucky too. He helped raise two daughters and then gained two more sons when Ken and Ken came along.

Ta Dad. We love you heaps!

Dad with his boys

Ken keeps abreast of the times

Spotted Dick

Ken's Farm Quiz, p.71:

1. Spring
2. Border collie, German beardie
3. Hammering metal
4. Pig farmer
5. Shearing sheep
6. Tupping
7. Safety strap on a saddle
8. Separating the cream from the milk
9. Through their nose
10. Angora (goat and rabbit)

Scores:

0 - 4 Never leave home
5 - 7 Halfway to being a farmer
8 - 10 Never come to town

Answers To Ken's Brain Stumper pp. 74–75:

bloody	oars	ray of	set
gorgeous	bestmates	sunshine	red
camp	lead role	gelt	pub
giday	aphanite	tart	see
daylight	mother	boss	ilk
friend	herd	eligible	elk
post	pink	roast	add
horse	ease	grease	dog
rose	sex appeal	henhouse	tea
bore	gadgets	aotearoa	dad
loans	taro	horns	bachelor
snores	taut	lake	

Ken's Secret Message:

Lady In Pink

Gingham's Country Music Quiz p. 102:

1. 'D.I.V.O.R.C.E.'
2. 'Sliver threads and golden needles'
3. 'Put another log on the fire'
4. 'The pub with no beer'
5. 'Green, green grass of home'
6. 'The gambler'
7. 'Seven Spanish angels'
8. 'Mama, don't let your babies grow up to be cowboys'
9. 'It's crying time again (you're gonna leave me)'

Prue And Dilly's Crossword pp.82-83:

S	O	C	I	E	T	Y	■	J	E	T
■	D	■		A	T	■		■	O	
C	A	L	O	R	I	C	■		S	
A	T	■	L	■		H	O	M	E	S
P	L	Y	■	C	A	T	■	I	■	
■	A	■	F	O	S	S	I	L	S	
A	N	■	A	■	A	■		L	■	
T	■	U	■	P	■	W	I	L	L	
I	■	N	I	■	F	■	O	■		
C	H	A	M	P	A	G	N	E	■	
A	■	E	■	A	■	T	E	A	R	S
C	H	A	N	G	E	■	T	I	R	E
C	A	R	■	E	N	D	■	R	■	X
U	■	T	■	T	■	S	E	T	■	
S	C	A	R	C	E	■		A	■	
T	O	T	E	■	R	E	T	U	R	N
O	■	T	A	R	T	■		N	O	
M	E	A	D	■	A	■	S	■	I	T
E	■	C	■	I	R	O	N	S	■	
D	■	K	I	L	N	■	S	O	H	O

Photo Credits:

Wherever possible we have credited the photographers who have contributed to our book. All other photographs The Topp Twins archive.

Barbara Thomson – p.60
Candid Camera Studies (Ham.) LTD – p.15
Melanie Church – pp. 32-33, 36-37, 61, 67, 113
Arani Cuthbert – pp. 68, 71, 81, 84, 100, 116
Andrew Hardy – p. 89
Peter Janes – pp. 34, 40–41, 49, 64, 80
Shona McCullagh – pp. 101, 114
Mary Massara – pp. 125, 128
Pete Molloy – p. 111
Nikki Pearson – pp. 62, 124
Sally Tagg – pp. 25, 26, 28, 35, 39, 44–45, 48–49, 50, 52, 54, 56–57, 70, 72–73, 76–77, 91, 93, 95, 97, 104–5, 115

Answers Page

Camp Mother & Camp Leader head off on another exciting adventure.

The End